Mother Mary's Final Message

Dr. Ralph B. White, M.Sc.D.

with

Erna M. White

Published by White Light Publishing

P. O. 499

Hazelwood, NC 28738-0499

Published by White Light Publishing
P. O. Box 499
Hazelwood, NC 28738-0499

Library of Congress Catalog Card Number 97-90666

ISBN: 0-9651085-1-1

Manufactured in the United States of America

DEDICATION

This book is dedicated to my beloved wife, Erna Maria, without whose assistance this book could not have been written. Also to the several special Angels for asking that this book be written, and giving freely of their time and effort to help us make it happen.

ACKNOWLEDGMENTS

Many thanks to the advanced students of this meditation for their dedication and assistance. Special thanks are given to advanced students Sharon Sparkman and Gregory Davies for their continued assistance and dedication to this work.

FOREWORD

A unique meditation enables us to bring Mother Mary's message to the world.   It has taken some students to the level where they can make personal contact with certain of the guides and angels, and interact with them with all senses functioning perfectly at that level.

While in this meditation, contact with the powerful angels at this level of consciousness becomes perfect and complete.   In addition to their special messages for the good of humanity, much of the information contained in these meditations, comes from Mother Mary's and the other angels' special instructions to Christina, while I listen to the entire process.

I led this advance student to the level that brought her into meditative contact with the special angels, and then monitored the contact, listened to the messages, and wrote them almost verbatim on the pages of this book.

In so doing, the actual thoughts and words flowing from the angels' mind into Christina's, are presented herein with the exact shade of meaning that accompanied the original thoughts.   All messages are as accurately presented as the human mind can understand that of an angel.

Although each stands alone, this book, **Mother Mary's Final Message,** completes what is really a trilogy.   The first two books, **Cosmic Fire, and Meditation Breakthrough For the Western World,** explain all that went on before and the events leading up to the present.   For information, send your request, either post-card or letter, to the publisher,

The purpose of these messages come from the concern and love of Mother Mary for every living person on earth. Assisting her in this project are several of the other angels who work with her at that level. They work in perfect harmony with a Divine Plan that is part of Universal Law, or the Natural Laws of the Universe.

They tell me that humanity, or man, does not understand that his gift of free-will carries with it an obligation to bring the total person to the highest level of perfection. The Divine Plan does not limit it to that of the physical, which is the lowest level of consciousness. For it to be perfect, it has to include the Mind and the Spirit.

These messages were created by the angels to give us an individual method to learn who we are, where we came from, and show us a way back. It can be used at our own leisure and in private. No one else needs to know unless the meditator wishes to share these experiences with like-minded friends and acquaintances.

The actual thoughts and concerns of Mother Mary and some of the other angels come alive on the pages of this book. Try to picture them in your mind as Christina speaks the words that breathe life into their ideas. See the pictures, hear the messages from the lips of the immortal angels who lived lives such as ours on earth long ago. They know us better than we know ourselves. Feel the impact these messages have on your plans for the future.

From the personal advice they give Christina, remember that the facts they give her can improve the lives of every person on earth. For they are truths about existence in the Angelic Realm, a world of peace and plenty that is only a single dimension separate from our own.

In the meditation we practice, we find the path back to Creation. Within it, we gain access to that dimension in the blissful state of awareness it gives us. We go in spirit to that promised land, share sensations of pure joy that we find impossible to attain in any other method we have found.

Most of all, they give us the true story of Creation, take us on guided tours of their worlds, and show us how those of us who follow this path will eventually exist throughout eternity.

It is a story that has never been completely told. I have never heard or read anything that can even remotely compare with actually seeing so many inhabitable planets that are waiting our coming. An untold number of them are ripe for the harvest.

From what I have seen, there must be billions of such planets. Civilizations from other worlds have claimed some of them for their own. No such thing as a shortage exists. Within the mighty Cosmos. More galaxies come into existence on a regular basis, each eventually containing millions of such worlds.

Most of this information comes from the minds of the angels and is contained in their messages as given to us through the mind of Christina.

In the messages that follow, details of life in their own realm come to us automatically as a by-product of their conversations. At other times, they tell us directly all the information we need to know.

In one instance, they tell us that highly-advanced individuals from some of the planets described above will contact us and show us how we can attain the same level of perfect existence as theirs, and reap rewards beyond our fondest dreams.

We can hasten the coming of that event if more people will join us in what we have already accomplished. In fact, we already have a home-study course in this method. Again, for information contact our publisher.

Often in these messages, the angels tell us their fears for our future here on earth. They tell us that we can correct some of the imbalance our life-style has created upon our planet, but we will have to change the way we use and abuse earth's natural resources.

Christina has been selected as their spokesperson, and asked to relay the following series of messages to every person on earth who cares to listen. If enough of us heed the warnings they give us, and join with us in what we are already doing, we can make enough difference to begin the necessary correction.

If we can make that correction we will then have a longer period of time to discover what we are doing wrong, and how we can return to Creation's plan for us being here on earth in the first place.

If we never awaken to the real purpose of our existence, the natural laws of cause-and-effect will run its course. The imbalance will continue, and life on this planet, as we know it, will eventually cease.

Those who join us in this meditative contact will have found the way. They learn how to make the contact and live in this special world for long periods of time, amid the hundreds of benefits and solutions this knowledge provides.

The angels tell us, one additional benefit outweighs all of the others. Those who reach the highest level of awareness in this method learn how to cross and recross at will the dimensional lines that separate our worlds.

Although that journey now occurs in the spiritual, when the need arises, they have a simple method of making the transition. They need only to break the connection with their present reality, and remain in that highest realm for an eternity.

The following statement comes from Christina, Mother Mary's chosen spokesperson. Spoken from the height of a powerful meditation, while in intense contact with the above angel, she describes the location in which contact is made, and imparts a wealth of information at the same time.

"This location is here for everyone. Our souls could learn much more and evolve much higher while we are still on our side of existence in the physical body and visit here as often as we can. This could be to our advantage when we finally return here forever. Then we can go to even higher levels."

We learn many facts from this one statement: this meditation can take one spiritually to the angelic realm, that anyone who wishes can learn this meditation and reach this level, if they do they can evolve much higher while still on the physical level. Afterwards, they can <u>return</u> to the angelic realm, and move even higher from that celestial plane of existence.

Approximately ninety percent of this book contains actual conversations such as the above, with Mother Mary and some of the other angels. As all of these angelic messages flow from them to the mind of Christina, consider the wealth of little-known information about their world you hold in your hands.

In addition, consider the importance of their messages to us, and the impact this knowledge will have on our lives. When we <u>know</u> what really awaits us in the future, we are much better prepared to actually live and enjoy the present. And all of this is made possible in a personal meditation, created by immortal angels, and dedicated to those of us on this planet who are driven by an intense desire to find the real <u>TRUTH.</u>

Mother Mary had asked me earlier to bring one of the more advanced students to this level. She wanted to make personal contact with such a person. When Christina made contact, she had found the messenger she wanted.

In addition to Mother Mary, other angels of the group working with us often came during these contacts and added their own messages to those of Mother Mary. The names of a few of those you will meet follow:

Mataji, Spiritual custodian of this special meditation,
  and for many years my own personal teacher.

Mirva, Mataji's sister.

Tschen Li, Tibetan Lama and physician, my earthly
  teacher, and now my angelic guide.

Joshua, my childhood guide, and still my teacher.

The Archangel Raphael, healing angel and teacher.

The Archangel Michael, working with Joshua and
  Tschen Li, on special assignment.

Jesus, the Christ, in support of his mother and humanity.

The Master Healer, Temple of Lights guide and teacher.

The Supreme Master. (Need I say more?)

The information that follows comes from the lips and minds of the angels mentioned above, and possibly a few others not listed.

It has made such a profound impact on my entire existence, my only purpose for remaining here is to bring this message to the attention of every living person on earth who cares to listen.

I look forward to the day when I will make my final ascension to that beautiful location, loose the bindings that keep me earthbound and remain in that paradise forever.

Sooner than you think, it just might be necessary.

           Ralph B. White

CONTENTS

Chapter I

In the Beginning

The coming of the night blended perfectly with the tranquil vibrations surrounding us. Christina's subdued weeping might have been seen as a contrast, but I knew they were tears of gladness. I watched her with mixed feelings of concern and joy: Concern with her physical stress, and joy over her unexpected breakthrough into the highest spiritual levels of our meditation.

She sat near me, barely visible in the semi-darkness of the room. Her tear-filled eyes reflected the rapture of her soul from opening the final door into the highest levels of awareness. It had just come to her for the first time ever, at the height of this special meditation that can be easily learned by anyone interested in making contact with the masters and angels.

Christina had just made the final breakthrough into the Angelic Realm, the abode of the Masters and Angels. And in that opening moment, one of the most revered of all angels, the mother of Jesus, had contacted and greeted her with an overwhelming, unconditional love.

Christina had studied a special meditation with me for many years. She knew its many possibilities. During that time, her love for Mother Mary, which had begun in child-hood, had grown to a very high level. However, spiritual contact with the Holy Mother had never been considered possible.

At the height of the meditation, Mother Mary made contact with Christina, called her "my child," and uttered a few words of welcome. Christina recognized her soft voice instantly. She became speechless in the intense emotion of the moment. Her tears came from the joy of this special contact. The overwhelming emotion continued. She remained unable to speak.

In the long moments that followed, the gentle mind of Mother Mary found my own and established contact. She had followed my progress over the long years of my study with the Master, Tschen Li, and the Angelic Masters, Mataji and Mirva, who had taught me this amazing meditation that, under their custody, had been millions of years in the making.

They called it the Masters' (or Angels') Meditation, and had taught it with limited success to some of the most brilliant minds of the past civilizations on planet earth. Yet it is a simple method, easy to use by everyone, with powerful results beyond all comparison.

Contact with the mind of that great lady led my thoughts back to our many communications. It also disclosed a possible reason for her interest in my progress during that time. She now manifested great concern over what she called earth's increasing patterns of devolution in human life. Negativity rapidly replaced spirituality, and created an imbalance that could easily lead to disaster and destruction.

The mind that held my own so gently came alive. She said, "Now you know why I told you earlier that this could be my last message to mankind. That is the reason we have chosen Christina as my spokesperson. After she gets over the surprise of my appearance, with her simple faith and great love, her concern will lead many people to listen to my messages. Then enough people will join with us to make the difference.

"A paradise of inhabitable planets are waiting for the awakening of earth's people, and we are ready to assist them find their way. We don't understand why so many choose to turn away from the simple path of returning to this level with all it has to offer. Here they can attain what has been called life everlasting with all its many possibilities.

"If we cannot awaken enough of them to the truth, their only reward will be death, to the planet first, and then to themselves. Yet it need not happen. We still have time to correct the imbalance. However, even that depends upon how quickly we can attract enough of them to look within and find their higher selves. Only then can they come to this vibrational level where they can learn the real truth and possibly help many others that come after them."

In my long period of study with the angelic masters who gave me so much of their precious time, we often spoke of the difference between earth's people and those on other planets. They explained how our own attitudes grew out of a preoccupation with many physical pleasures and rewards to the exclusion of our spiritual growth and development.

Mother Mary points the finger of blame at no one. She will help us identify the cause of the imbalance, and offer the only solution we now have that can help us make the correction before it becomes too late. Having lived on this planet for a lifetime, she understands us perfectly. We are fortunate that her love for us is so great, she is now making this final effort to help us save ourselves from destruction.

Of course, the change in the attitude of our people will have to come first. Then a period of time must occur while our minds and bodies are purified enough to make the journey into the higher levels of existence. Following that period of correction will come the necessary awareness that can lead us to a blissful life in a special paradise located in these higher levels of life everlasting.

Mother Mary knows there are already many people

seeking workable answers. Since she was one of the angels
who helped fashion this meditation out of the natural laws
of the universe, she knows that it is built upon the sound
foundation of Creation's Principles. She knows that it will
work, and is aligning her voice and influence with that of
the other angels and masters

Over the long period of time encompassing mankind's
existence on earth, man-made laws and social customs
during those times allowed only a few people to make the
ascension into the higher levels of existence. The real path
back to Creation remained carefully concealed.

Still others have been deliberately held back through
ignorance of the path's existence, or involuntary servitude
by whatever name it has existed over the ages. Some have
hopelessly succumbed to the temptations and luster of
earthly attractions, power and greed. In the final analysis,
as a matter of natural law, any decision to go within and
find the way back is entirely up to each individual.

We still waited for the newly awakened soul the angels
called Christina, to adjust to the unexpected elevation to this
extremely high spiritual level. The deep love she held in her
heart since childhood for the mother of Jesus had attracted
Mother Mary's attention, and caused her to come to us in
this special meditation. We felt the sincerity of Christina's
love as she continued weeping softly.

The gentle mind of this Great Lady still cradled my own.
She said, "I think it's better that I withdraw for now and let
you take her back slowly to her world of reality. Over the
next few weeks, bring her back to this location several
times. I will come to her each time. She is so easy to
contact and will soon become the bearer of my messages to
mankind.

"I know that she will do well. Thank her for her love and support. I love her very much and will visit her often." She slowly faded from my view, but the meditation continued. With the assistance of other angels, Mataji and Mirva had brought us to this location. They are our principal teachers, and had taught us how to reach this level of contact with them. They are preparing Christina to bring other students to this special planet where contact and communication with several of the angels and masters is easily possible.

In Christina's earlier study of this method, its powerful benefits helped her overcome many personal problems and conflicts that had marred her life. Once she accepted the spiritual truth contained in this meditation, she became an excellent student and her life began to work. Our teachers loved her for her sincerity and determination.

Her presence at this high level attests to the degree of her advancement and ability. It is because of her progress to this high vibrational level that Mother Mary has chosen Christina to bring these, her final messages, to the attention to all who want to hear. For she believes that if these messages are not heeded, much of human life on earth will be lost.

The planet earth, once called the Pearl of the Universe by the angels, will not cease to exist. The glowing luster that radiated outward from its surface, and gave it its name, will be gone.

No longer able to fully sustain life as we know it, selected people will be gathered in small groups. With special instructions from the angels, these groups will live in small, habitable communities. There they will live and grow under the loving guidance of the angels. Those that we and others help teach, will then be guided by the angels, and given the skills to lead and help them through this transitional period. There they will live in peace, harmony and love, while waiting for the dawning of the new world of peace and love the angels have promised us.

As for earth, it will lie fallow through many succeeding generations. Too late for those who refuse to see, the passage of time will bring it back to the point that it will live again, and support other generations when all is ready.

The angels taught us how to make this ascension at will. They have told us, as well as others, how to offer this opportunity to those who want to work with us and wish to experience the wonders of the angelic realm, and the wisdom that comes with it.

Excitement continues to increase among those who work with us. They now know that they too can learn to communicate with some of the many angels and masters who teach us at that level. As many continue to grow and teach these lessons to others, they will attain the same ability, and begin doing it on their own.

Christina had awakened. A sheepish smile told me more than words. She had closed her eyes again, apparently in very deep thought. She had many things to ponder before the final reawakening.

Still in the full glory of our celestial contact, my own teachers had much to tell me before I finally drifted into the rapture of a blissful sleep.

Chapter II

The Angels' Promise.

Several months had passed. It had required many more meditations before Christina overcame the deep emotions created by the overwhelming effect of Mother Mary's presence. To her credit, Christina valiantly fought back the tears as she tried to speak, but her choking voice still refused to function. The Great Lady seated before her continued to send her messages of understanding and love. Slowly the tears gave way to smiles and expressions of happiness. Mother Mary had the contact of her choice. Christina would now bring the vision and wisdom of this revered angel to the people of our world in her simple way as these messages came into her mind while in the deep state of meditative contact.

We were told that not every word would come from Mother Mary as the primary source. Other masters and angels of our group assisted us in attaining that high level of contact. They would occasionally join us with their energy, and their own messages, thus enhancing the value of the information.

Time became an important factor. The angels wanted this information made available to the people of our world as quickly as possible. They urged me to hasten the pace of my writing. Although they made no reference to a date or time, every action on their part revealed extreme concern.

I had lived in personal contact with angels for a long time. As they opened my mind to the natural laws of the universe, my increasing awareness of the progressive deterioration of our planet and its inhabitants concerned me greatly. The human part of my mind had refused to accept any parallel between the extinction of a bird or an animal and that of humanity itself. After I learned of the law of natural selection, I found myself concerned that we might be next.

To understand why the angels do not use their full power, you only have to look within and open yourself to these natural laws that govern the universe. There you will see that you have free will, free will to return to the Creator from whence you came or to suffocate in continued ignorance of that law. It remains your personal decision alone. In other words, it is all up to you.

The properly motivated human mind can accomplish miracles. If then it looks within and finds the other half, its spiritual connection, it will have reached a level where the angels could teach it the secrets of their world. Only then could it become whole again. While there are other methods of making contact, to the best of my knowledge, their own method would be the best and quickest one to study, for it is their own. Under the unconditional love of the Eternal Presence, you know it is untainted by human greed.

In her messages, Mother Mary referred to this as *My Book.* Since she had volunteered to be the primary source, none of the others offered any objection. Of course, in the working relationships among angels, every individual action always worked in harmony with that of the entire group, because they were of one mind. It is not too important as to who brings this message, but how quickly we can bring it to our world.

I remembered the many years my masters and I had led Christina into ever higher levels of spiritual contact. They had been productive years, and we all shared her joy as she developed spiritually and moved into the highest levels of contact, without her even being fully aware of it.

Having been party to the angels' plans for years, I now

had someone to personally share the wisdom of the angels with me and make my work easier. The angels spoke of many others that would also come to our assistance in time. How could anyone ever be lonely in paradise. The joy of working with them and sharing their friendship with others, brought untold pleasure into our own lives.

Among the many personal benefits derived from their association, instant contact became the most treasured. A mere thought enabled me to penetrate the dimensional barrier between our worlds, and attain immediate contact with that special group of angelic masters.

Mother Mary's messages that flow through Christina's mind to you in the following chapters, will all be brought to you as precise as possible. In each of these sessions, they will be taking her into special meditations leading to the higher levels of consciousness. While there, she will be in contact with the Holy Mother and other angels.

I personally can suggest of only one successful method of easily contacting these high level spiritual beings. It is the masters' and angels' own special meditation. It bears their own name. The Masters' Meditation. Mataji once told me it had been with them from almost the beginning of time.

Although contact is made in the first meditation, there are several natural levels of meditations necessary to work through before one reaches the level of contact where easy communications exist between those of the angelic realm and our own. There they can reach us at that level with ease.

Sometimes they reach down through the levels and touch someone and give them special assistance. In their wisdom, they know that person's destiny and make the extra effort to help them achieve it.

Some people pause in their ascent, then later come back to the path. For there is nothing else on earth that offers the same benefits and pleasure as living in the Divine Presence and under the personal protection of the Creator..

Christina has studied this meditation with me for many years. She has become quite proficient without being aware of it. Mother Mary is her main contact, but we have also had similar contact with many other angels.

In almost all of the contacts, in addition to their messages, they have requested that we train others to learn this meditation and ultimately become message bearers similar to Christina.

We begin the messages in the next chapter. Each contact will come after Christina has advanced through this meditation to an extremely high level of consciousness. We know that it is our spiritual consciousness that has made this advancement, yet it often seems that our own physical bodies have accompanied us to this special meeting place.

We are on a planet in the angelic realm. Only a single dimension separates it from that of our own. Yet they might as well be light years apart, for such contact can best be attained with the special meditative method.

We meet in an awe inspiring location. It is situated on that beautiful planet in the angelic realm, that could almost be a duplicate of planet earth before the arrival of mankind.

The angelic realm embraces all of the massive extent of what they call the Cosmos. All but the planet earth, which seems to be under some kind of a quarantine of its own making.

While this book brings you many profound revelations of the angels, making you aware of immediate problems that need attention, that could be solved in many simple ways. In bringing us their messages, many details of their existence are revealed to us as a simple by-product. Some of this information may differ slightly from that previously revealed by various denominational teachings. It is our purpose only to bring to you the angels' messages as they are revealed to us in the purest way. The angels themselves tell us that in finding and using their own meditational method of contact, we are automatically made aware of their lifestyle and abilities.

Mother Mary answered that question wisely in one of Her revelations when she said, "I am ready to communicate with anyone who merges the spiritual with the physical and moves to a vibrational level high enough for me to contact them."

She and other highly evolved angels are anxious to speak to anyone who learns to attain their level of consciousness. Christina, I, and many others have promised and devoted the remainder of our lives to bringing the angels' messages to our world.

We are also prepared to teach this meditation to as many as we can, within the limits of our capacity. In so doing, we just might save our planet from an untimely end, and as many of our people who care to study with us.

Prepare yourself to actually journey to another world that is located amid the thousands of habitable planets located in the angelic realm. Totally experience the wonders of travel to those worlds, as you listen to Christina's voice bringing Mother Mary's messages.

Allow your five senses to come alive and experience the many wonders found on this typical planet where the angels live amid the many wonders of everlasting life. Hold these pictures in your mind as the voices of angels prepare you to take your rightful place in their midst when you, too, find your way back to that level of everlasting life.

Remember that as Christina speaks, she does so out of the elevated level of an expanded consciousness. Sensations of rapture and bliss hold her in their gentle arms. She is surrounded by angels, and speaks their messages for the benefit of everyone on earth.

Mother Mary's First Message

With this chapter, frequent visits to the special celestial location begin. Under the guidance of angels, Christina will advance rapidly and soon reach a level enabling her to complete the entire procedure on her own. Mother Mary has directed that I lead her into the contact, then allow Christina to tell the details of the messages.

The series of contacts are important to the future of our planet and its inhabitants. Mother Mary and the angels want *Her Book* finished and published as soon as possible, with the assistance of others, I will put the messages into book form. My familiarity with the content will help me complete my part faster and more easily.

We have just completed ascension to this special planet. Listen to the words of Christina telling what she sees and feels prior to and upon entering the special meeting place.

"I am nearing a large, delightful meadow. I have been told this is called the valley of tranquillity. It is in between the temple and the crystal homes surrounded with beautiful mountains on both sides. I love to sit here and look at the deep blue lake. It is so crystal clear that if you sit right in front of it you can see your reflection on top of the lake like a mirror image.

"The mountains are right behind this lake and they radiate a glowing energy, as well as protection. It is such a special place, and I always feel that I have to sit here for a few minutes, immersed in sensations of tranquillity.

"I know that this lake has a special meaning. It is just the deepest blue I have ever seen, and it is totally still. But when I stand in front of it, I feel that I can merge myself with the lake and never feel wet. Sensations of peace reach

out and embrace me, like waking up from a long sleep, when
in reality, only a few seconds have elapsed.
   "There is total harmony and balance within and without.
I am hearing music coming out of the three crystal steeples,
as I am walking towards the temple. I can't really tell if it is
made of stone or cement or what. There is no glass evident,
just a very solid building. No windows.
   "The door is already open, and many (angels) are there
to receive me with such love and happiness. I feel a sense of
equality here. Everything, everyone is the same. They are
filled with such love, such happiness, and nothing else
matters.
   "They are happy that I come here. Not so much happy
for me but for my soul, happy that my soul can advance
much more while I am still attached to this physical body.
They always mention that, for they feel it is so very
important for my Spiritual growth.
   "They know that the knowledge I am bringing back to
the physical and sharing with others is important for our
planet. They wish they could have had the same chance
while many were still on earth. Now they have to wait for
their next earthly assignment. They are so kind, so caring,
so understanding.
   "These light beings are slowly escorting me to a front
seat. There is something like a stage in front of me. It is
well lit in the center, but everything else around here is in
subdued darkness. It is very quiet."
   "In my contact with them, they were expressing regret
that they were not able to attain the level I am on. In their
contact with me, they were also regretting that none of those
they worked with had ever attained my level of experience
or understanding.

Christina continues. "I hear <u>Mother Mary</u> coming in. There is this special sound, the sweet aroma, and vibration. It is a lovely and gentle vibration."

She tells me, "Hello, my child. I am happy you have come back. Much more light has been spread around your planet. I am pleased that many of you are working together in this endeavor. However few people can reach that level in the beginning, yet each one that tries can make a difference. All they have to do is ask for help, and the whole universe can hear."

Christina said, "As I see it, life on our planet could be beautiful, but not until we treat this disease that is devouring us. This temple is filled with—I don't see them as angels. All I see is light beings like veils floating around. There is always a faint music in the background. It is such a beautiful surrounding. Mother Mary is smiling."

She tells me, "Your planet could be just as beautiful if you would only lift your vibrations to a higher level where negative thoughts cannot reach you. Then you would be surrounded with only pure and loving thoughts."

Christina said, "I feel so much love around me, it is just overwhelming."

Mother tells me, "I have to listen to anyone who needs my help. I will never turn anyone down. You are all my children as well children of the universe. You all have souls, and it is the soul in which I am very concerned, not so much the physical body."

Christina said, "She wants to be the mother of our souls, and to show us her love, but she can't do that unless we first asks her for help. Oh, what a beautiful thought."

Christina said, "I just sometimes feel, Mother, that you are doing so much for humanity and they do next to nothing for you."

"But you see," she tells me, "we have this unconditional love that you cannot ever understand while in the physical body. You can only hear my words, but you will never be able to understand just how deep unconditional love can be."

"I guess not." Christina said.

"Just remember," Mother Mary continued, "how my son suffered. and never one word of pain came out of his lips. That was also unconditional love and cannot ever be compared to how deep our unconditional love is."

"I find it difficult to visualize one of us suffering as he did," Christina said, "and doing this as unconditional love. It is totally unthinkable."

But she tells me, "This is one analogy that I can give you. That way you know what unconditional love we have for your planet and for humanity. He endured all this pain for humanity."

"Yes, I know," said Christina, "and I think it is about time that humanity recognized the sacrifice that he made and I think we all need to do our part, mainly to help humanity find a way back to where they came from and not becoming totally lost and devoured by the darkness."

Mother Mary is saying, "The only way for you to live in peace and harmony is by joining together and becoming this oneness through spiritual togetherness. Only then can you find peace on both levels. You must learn to overcome all the greed, power, jealousy, and everything else, for they did not exist when we were created.

"You were created in a spiritual image, but because of the free will you were given, you have made the wrong choices and these choices grew bigger, and have reached the point of saturation. It is like a bubble that is going to burst anytime.

"You need to increase your love and your spirituality. Only then can you work together to save humanity, only then can you rebuild into this new spiritual human being that you were destined to be from the very beginning.

'It does not matter how much you do or how little you connect or how little you practice spirituality as long as you do it. You all must join together for only then can you become strong, only then can you grow and only then can the Divine Plan work for it is very much integrated with all there is above and below."

Christina said, "I get the feeling that the Divine Plan is alive, and is feeling the pain."

And she tells me that, "Everything is alive! It is alive because of who created it!"

"Oh Mother, said Christina, "this is all so sad."

But she is smiling and telling me, "You see, my child, since you have started sharing your message, many have already opened and connected with us. So you see, we already see many rays of sunshine coming from your planet and this sunshine is overshadowing the darkness."

"Oh, that is lovely," said Christina.

"Yes," said Mother Mary, "but we need to get these rays to become stronger so that they can totally disintegrate the darkness and that is your job to tell what they should do."

"Of course, said Christina, "I will do all I can."

She tells me, "You have become so strong, my child, but you have only reached a small part of your real strength. You will always have our help, you will always have our love that is very much a part of you."

Christina said, "Oh, Mother Mary, you are so easy to talk to. I had no idea, now I know. You will talk with anyone who needs your help. We all have our part to do. It only takes a little time and effort.

"Mother is reaching out and holding my hand. I still can't handle this overwhelming love. Thank you so much for your message. This can be experienced by anyone who really wants to talk to Mother Mary."

Mother Mary said, "Just know that everyone has a soul. Once you open your soul to this higher vibrational level, everything is possible. Just to think positive thoughts, to do good deeds, to be loving and caring, is all that is needed. With these little deeds, you can lift your vibrational level. It is all so simple."

Christina said, "Oh, is this ever emotional! And I get this kind of a last thought."

She is saying, "It is only emotional because of your physical body, for you have not learned yet to deal with it. This is why you have to become stronger for then you can detach your emotions and know the reason why and rise above it and find great understanding and consolation within yourself.

"You must learn to think with your mind, after it has been opened to the realization that it is a part of the soul, and full contact between them has been established.

"It is at that moment of full contact that the human body comes fully alive and claims its birthright in the full harmony of the Creator's unconditional love.

"Healing of the physical body begins at that moment. You reached that level sometime ago. I watched the changes taking place within you. Knowing the promise you made when you came into this incarnation, I blessed you with my special energy and love, and waited for you to come to this level of communication."

Christina said, "Thank Heavens you waited. I couldn't remember my promise, but somehow I knew I had to wait. knowing that someone would eventually tell me what I had to do. When I think how easy you are to talk to almost blows my mind. Please keep the line of communication between us open. I will come back often. "She is moving slowly off to the right. Like a personal whisper from out of the distance, I hear a faint, 'I love you.' A personal message from a very special Lady, telling me good-bye from the distance. Who could ask for anything more?"

In the silence that followed, Mother Mary faded slowly from view. We continued to sit silently, still overwhelmed by the tremendous force of energy left lingering around us.

As hard as I may try, it is difficult for me to depict in mere words the dynamic force of energy brought to us by the mere presence of this great lady. That force continues to accelerate to unheard of levels as mental contact surges into vocal. All five senses come to life at the spiritual level. These and perhaps others we are not aware of, lifting our conscious awareness to ever higher spiritual levels.

In moments like these, spiritual serenity holds me in the arms of unconditional love. I have learned to carry these sensations back with me into the world of normal con-sciousness. They surround me in a beautiful aura of bliss. The lingering rapture touches the souls of others that come into our presence, making teaching this meditation easy and powerful.

With this, the beginning of many informational contacts with Mother Mary and other angels comes to a close. The intensity of the contacts grow stronger. Interspersed with special instructions for Christina and general instructions for everyone on earth, the revelations of the angels will continue to astound as well as enlighten you.

Chapter IV   **21**

They Request Our Help

The following meeting with <u>Mother Mary</u> and the other
celestial beings, brings out the general pattern for the angels'
communication with us. It contains their concern over our
overall abuse of planet earth, and what we should be doing
to correct it.

They see us robbing the planet of its abundance of
natural resources, enjoying everything we can use, and
carelessly returning the mountain of untreated residue to its
surface in a form that contains enough poison to ultimately
render it incapable of supporting our kind of life.

Their concern goes a lot further. They see us chiefly
concerned with the physical, the material side of existence,
with almost no concern for the spiritual. This leaves us in a
one-sided, unbalanced mode of existence where the soul, the
essence of life, is neglected or not even recognized.

Their purpose in making this contact is to correct this
imbalance while there is still time. Everyone reading this
book can profit from the information about the "other side,"
and their possible solution.

It is to this end that we bring you the angels' unconditional love for mankind, their willingness to assist, and
their wisdom as they suggest solutions that those of us who
are concerned can use for our own salvation as well as that
of our planet.

Christina and I have arrived at our favorite seats in the
Temple of Knowledge. Contact came easily, and Christina
is speaking.

"Mother Mary is very happy that I came back today.
She holds my hands so that I can feel her energy, then
perhaps I won't have to cry as much. It is all so very over-

whelming."

Mother Mary said, "I am glad that you have decided to help me. You will now be the person between us at this level and your physical level back on earth. You will have to take this responsibility very seriously. We cannot lose any more time. It is of extreme importance. Everyone you can reach must help you, and in turn us. The need is great. With enough help, we just might make the difference.

"Since you began telling others, I have already seen a little improvement for the better. It pleased us to see earth's vibrations getting a little stronger. That is always a good indication of change for the better.

"Using your vibrations you can help the others that work with you, and lift them into the higher vibrations that can improve the quality of their lives. In so doing, you can make the difference as they see the positive changes taking place in their own lives and that of the others around them.

"It is important to lift your own vibrations to these higher levels, because it separates you from the prevailing negativity that holds earth in its grip—a grip that's pulling it and you down into a bottomless black hole.

"And the vibrational level of the light you find at this high level is important, because it can help take you to this higher level whenever you wish. When you have reached this level, you will begin to hear, feel, see and reconnect with it. Once the connection is made, you have found your way back home again.

"I feel strongly about your finding this vibration again. I know how much it has helped you, and I know it will help many others reach the same level. Once they have reached it, they will feel so good about themselves, they will never want to fall back to the lower level again."

Christina said, "And then, we will have gained many more souls to help us. Those we have touched will finally realize they have found the higher level they were searching for all their lives, and didn't know how to get there."

Mother Mary said, "And you can help them by beginning with the light, and by asking all of your masters to touch the many souls on your planet that are seeking help, and to touch their minds and help them. Then they too will help us spread the light.

"It will have such a great effect, once they feel and see the higher vibrations. Once the higher vibrations are reached and they are surrounded by light at this vibrational level, they will hunger for even more.

"At that level. they are going to feel so good, the quality of their life will improve greatly. It will improve so much they will not ever want to lose it again.

"They will remember their former lives, the eternal tired feeling from struggling just to eke out a living, tired of fighting, tired of feeling miserable.

"They will compare it to the high level they have just reached. Because here is where they can feel good, where everything they touch just works out so well without them making a very big effort."

Christina said, "And Mother Mary is saying that if we continue on this level, that we will be able to reach many people. And she said it is never too late, never, never too late. We just have to keep at it. We have to be strong. We have to have such a great level of endurance, and she will be there for everyone who will ask her for help. She will not turn anyone down. She will be here for everyone."

She is saying, "I have an unmeasurable amount of love. A never ending amount of love for everyone."

Christina said, "Oh God, is that beautiful. Thank goodness I don't have to cry so much today. Thank <u>you</u> Mother Mary.

"She is so very happy that she can come through to me loud and clear and then I can interpret it to the best of my ability, and then share it with our people. She wants so much to help our planet. She loves our planet. She doesn't want anything to happen to us or our planet.

"This planet was created to be our paradise, but we didn't treat it very well. I know."

Christina continued, "I can hardly believe my eyes. I see the majestic figure of an angel who I think could only be <u>Jesus</u> coming in behind her. He is telling me that he is pleased that I am doing what I had promised. He is also telling me that much has already changed for the better since the last time! Whatever little progress we make can make a change, can make a difference. He is very pleased that it is begun,

"Even though I am just this one little girl. I have already made a difference."

And he tells me, "Everyone, no matter how small or how large can make a difference. If you can do it, everybody can do it. It doesn't matter how big, how short, how young, how old, or what color. It is not important.

"Everyone has a soul. And to attain this high level, they must get in touch with their soul. And through this contact, the soul will do whatever is necessary, whatever it needs to do. But it has to have the support from the physical body. The physical body, the mind and the soul must work together. One cannot properly function without the other."

Christina said, "Wow! They are thanking me. They are thanking me because I had the courage and wanted to come.

Yes, I know I should have done this a long time ago. They said it was never too late.

"Mother Mary is sitting just in front of me. My whole body feels very light, very still, very calm. How can I describe that. It feels so good. I mentally asked myself what will happen if we don't get enough people, what will happen to the world? Will she tell us the consequences of us not coming in great numbers? What would the consequence be?"

Mother said, "Then the inevitable will happen. Many have written, many have spoken about it, but none of them really know. None of them have any idea just how severe it will be, they cannot imagine. They have no idea, because this has never happened to this planet before. This will be a first.

"They can only think of it in a very small way. There is no way to measure. They are not evolved enough to measure. But she tells me not to think about that, but only to think of what we can do to right the wrong.

"She told me we have already made a difference since yesterday."

Christina said, "I was talking with her when I went for a walk earlier. I was standing on top of our mountain looking out across the village up to the sky and it came to me that I am already here on a little piece of paradise. That I am so grateful. I am so thankful, I am so humble."

"And she said everybody can feel like that, but they first have to look at our planet with different eyes and not have the wrong perception, and not look in the wrong direction. If they would look at our planet as a paradise, it can be a paradise again, but we cannot waste any more time."

Christina said, "Thank you Mother Mary. And she told

me to give her my hands. She wanted to hold my hands."
And she said, "You know I love you dearly. I have
known you a long time. But now the time for action has
come. We have so much to do."

Christina said. "I must be her spokesperson on our
planet, to receive all the messages from her here, and convey
them to our people on earth."

She tells me, "There is much darkness on your planet.
The light can't come through and you have to help. You
have to bring the light, otherwise you will all suffer terribly.
You must spread as much light as you can, and tell everyone
who is like-minded; they have to spread the light over the
planet. For the more light you spread, hopefully the darkness
will not catch up with you.

"You have to make headway, you must hurry. There is
very little time left. You must continue telling your people,
they have to spend more time just bathing the planet in light.
Whatever color you feel comfortable: white or gold or blue,
just put it in light. The darkness is consuming you.

"You can prevent some things, and those that are
spreading the light will continue to bring peace to your
planet and will help rebuild it. Don't ask for anything in
return, but you have to be devoted. If you are not devoted,
its not going to work."

Christina said, "She has been trying to reach many
people, but they lack the higher awareness to make contact!
They used their minds only for personal advantage rather
than use it to help our planet! They did not want to help
Mother Mary so therefore she is quite disappointed and sad.

"But she knows I will do it, because I made the promise
before I entered into this lifetime. For this, I bring a special
gift into this incarnation. She remembered my promise and

always hoped I would remember and come to them sooner. As with everyone on earth, I had free will and had to learn my lessons first. Now she is happy that I finally came."

Christina said, "Oh, it's hard! Many will join us, but we first have to convince them how serious this is! We have very little time to prepare."

"I asked her how much time. She said that was not important. We could not measure it anyway. We have to do everything we can <u>now</u>."

Christina said, "I will do all I can, and I will ask whoever I know that is willing to help, if they will help. She wants so much to help us, but so far her efforts have been fruitless!

"Nobody wanted to take her advice! They didn't want to follow through because it was too much effort! She is telling me now this is enough, that I will not get that emotional the next time because I will be able to handle this energy better from now on. Oh, thank you.

"She is leaving me now. I just feel like there is a cool breeze going the other way. Oh, she is so full of love! Why don't people want to help her."

"Her voice came from the distance. She said, "Because they were always pulled down for materialistic reasons. They are seeking things they don't even need, when they already have more than they can use."

Christina said, "I can't see why they want so much. I have all I want already. So why shouldn't I do this work that is so necessary. I am not looking for anything else! I don't need any clothes. I don't need any jewelry, I don't need anything! Why can't our people feel their real need is to regain contact with their souls? Why don't they know?"

The answer came quickly, "Because they don't want to know."

Christina asked, "Whoever told me that?"

Mirva appeared and said, "They don't want to know. They are too busy with unnecessary things that are happening on your earth. They don't realize that most of them are about to fall into this big black hole.

"Yet, there are many people out there who want to help, but they don't know what to do. It will be difficult to reach those people.

"I am being told that in meditation we are to ask our Masters and Angels to please contact all these people, all these souls that are highly evolved to do this work, and the message will touch their minds.

"That's the only way we can reach so many of them, because we don't even know who they are. We don't know where they are, but the angels know. Of course, and they will want to work with us and help us.

"Why didn't we think **of** that before? Because I never asked. Okay. My face is so wet, I've got to dry my face. Oh, I can't handle any more. With all this energy flowing through me, it is so hard to think, but somehow they always help me to connect and understand."

Still in the deep state of meditation that brought us here, Christina and I sit quietly in the lingering aura of the Holy Mother's presence. The great love of the Creator that fills this planet holds us blissfully in its arms.

Our minds filled with wonder, we will have much information to consider before returning to the world of normal consciousness.

Chapter V **29**

Windows of the Soul

Christina and I have just completed the spiritual ascension to this level. She tells us of her experiences.

She said, "I am floating slowly over some mountain ranges. They took me some place else today, but now I am summoned to go and visit Mother Mary, and I don't want to be late.

"I see lots of stars out tonight. In the darkened night they twinkle and glisten brightly. Some seem to be so close, and stationed almost in midair. It is as if they are not all the way up in the sky, and I could almost reach up and touch them. They are like tiny dots of light, hanging in suspension. They seem so very close, like bits of silver paper. I know they are real because I feel the energy and warmth. They are very real and I think I can float up to them and can probably touch them.

"What a magnificent picture. I have never been up here at night. I can hear beautiful music coming from the stars. It is like they are having a concert among themselves, like they are celebrating. What a sight. I wish I could spend more time here but I have to go in. I know that she is waiting for me. The urge to touch one of them remains. Then, again, it's best that I don't. I might even get burned, and that wouldn't be good.

"The door to the temple seems heavier than usual tonight. It's difficult to push open. There are not many here, just a few. Where did they all go to? There are only five or six (angels) floating around. I wonder why. But they are so happy to see me.

"They are telling me that this is a special meeting and this is the reason only a few of the special ones are present. I am now sitting in my chair and waiting.

"There is Mirva, she is coming towards me and extending her arms, at the same time telling me mentally to touch her hands so that I can feel her energy.

And she tells me, "You know little sister, I am very, pleased that you have come this far. You have made good progress, and that makes all of us happy. Not everyone makes such quick progress the way you have, but of course you are special.

"You know that you are special, you have advanced so quickly since your breakthrough. Look at what you are feeling and sharing. Not everyone can do that. Remember that I am always with you no matter how little or how much help you need, I will always be there."

Christina said, "Yes, I know, and for that I am very grateful."

Mirva said, "I, as well as many other angels, will always be there for you,. In turn, you must also be there for us."

Christina said, "Of course, what more can I do?"

Mirva continued, "You need to fulfill this one project, this one task, for it is very important. And we will always be there whenever you need us, Because for now you are the only one that can do it. Soon you will receive your benefits, once this is completed. Perhaps this will help you understand much better.

"My sisters and I have been working very closely with the few of you special children."

Christina said, "I presume you mean Mataji and me as your sisters."

"Yes," Mirva said, "Just like you, we have been sisters from a long time ago. This is why we are so close and you are very dear to us. You are so very beautiful."

Christina said, "Of course you mean my soul, right."

Mirva said, "Of course. You can envision your body as beautiful all you want to. But you see, without the beauty of your soul, your body cannot be beautiful either! Therefore, let this beauty shine through your body with your soul. Once you do, it will be recognized.

"It is there for everyone, but not everyone can achieve that. You cannot have a beautiful smile unless your soul smiles through you. You cannot have beautiful eyes, unless your soul speaks through your eyes."

"Oh, Mirva," Christina interjected.

And she tells me, "You know that!"

Christina said, "She is making me look at her eyes and her eyes are almost nothing but silver glistening almost like stars, They have a twinkle in them and shining like silver."

She tells me, "This is the smile of my soul that I beam out through my eyes, and this is how you will be recognized, and you are also aware of that.

"In time to come, this will become even stronger where they will know that you are not only special, but you are very much connected with us!

"Guard this soul of yours very well. Treasure it, for this is all you have. You cannot share it with anyone who is not on equal level with you, for it will take away from its beauty."

Christina said, "I somehow feel you are telling me this for a special reason."

And she tells me, "Yes. And you will know one day. You will know for this is the only way you will grow. You will become strong and then you will be able to achieve anything you want to."

Christina said, "As Mirva moves to the back of the stage,

now I see <u>Mataji</u> coming.

"Oh, God, her eyes are just—they are both of them just—it is almost like a magnet. I almost cannot even look at them any more."

She is telling me, "This is the power of the soul that will become stronger and stronger as you reach higher levels. You will have these eyes too. Then will you be recognized as a very special person. This will be your acceptance. They will acknowledge you for who and what you are. They will know you are a special soul."

"Why are the eyes so important?"

Mataji said, "The eyes are the windows of the soul. Even those that are not on your path will know that there is something special!"

Christina said, "This is why I saw the stars outside earlier. Now I see stars in your eyes. Oh, how lovely! But what is the real meaning to all this? It comes to me like the way I am taken with their eyes, with the power of their eyes, yet there is so much love and gentleness, sweetness and kindness. It is overpowering, and I am filled with awe."

And she tells me, "You can have it one day too, but you cannot ever abuse it. With this power in your eyes you can demand discipline, attention, respect. These things you will need one day, little one. Your eyes are beautiful and you know they are glowing for you have been told."

"I guess you don't miss much do you?"

She is telling me, "We only miss those things that are unimportant! You will have the power with your eyes to penetrate other eyes and you will know if they are truthful or trying to deceive you, or if they are deceitful. So pay much attention to eyes for they will turn their eyes down if they are untruthful. If they are truthful, they have no fear of your eyes for you will know."

Christina said, "Mataji is now walking slowly to the back of the stage.

"Mother Mary is coming in. She has a rose in her hand, and she is handing it to me again."

She tells me, "I bring you my love."

Christina said, "Oh, Mother how could I not love you. How could anybody not love you. You are love. You are everything that means love!"

She tells me, "As you have heard from your sisters, this is very important. Soon you will have a problem, but not really a problem because everything has been arranged. Everything will be arranged, all you have to do is to follow our path.

"As you come more and more to this hall of education, you will become stronger, you will be guided. You will know exactly what to do, but of course you always have free will my child."

Christina said, "But why wouldn't I want to do what you want me to do? There is nothing on our planet that can even equal, remotely what I have here, what I feel here, who I am here. It is not even a question."

Christina said, "She always smiles at me like 'I knew what you would say in answer.'"

She said, "Of course you know! There is so much work to be done. So many problems to be solved. You need much energy, you need harmony, you need balance and you need reinforcement. You shall have that on all levels!

"Do not forget. Soon the battle will begin—the spiritual battle has already begun! There is much intensity on your planet because of the lower parts. The darker parts of your planet are very much aware of the spiritual battle and there is much tension."

Christina said, "And we are picking this up."

And she tells me, "Of course you are. This is why you need to become very strong. You need to work together on all levels. You need to support each other on all levels for they will attack, especially when you are very vulnerable! Be always aware for they want to attack. They know that souls like you and others are on our side, and that they want to destroy any opposition they can.

"Do not let anything come between you! Always be aware for it will intensify in a very subtle way. Do not ever lose sight, and do not get out of harmony and balance because of pettiness! There is no time and no room for that. You now have to deal with greater problems, and they are getting to be difficult.

"The forces of darkness are moving closer and closer little one. You have to be very mindful of their presence. This is my message tonight. All of you that are involved in this are quite vulnerable right now.

"Guard yourselves well! Let the windows of your soul search for these dark shadows. They cannot tolerate the energy that you beam out of your eyes. They fear these eyes. This is why you must become strong!"

Christina said, "I see. In other words it is other human beings like we are that are these dark shadows."

She said, "Of course they are. There are also the thought forms these humans create. And there will be more and more of them coming closer and closer. Be very much aware of it. Search very carefully for your soul cannot make a mistake. Your soul will tell you. And your eyes will be able to penetrate, for the darkness cannot hide from you.

"But of course if you are not quite sure, always connect

with us, for we are very sure, and you will know in an instant and you will also know how to deal with them."

Christina said, "In other words this is a special warning for all of us."

She said, "Yes, my child. It is also a learning lesson. They will become stronger and stronger, and you must be aware of it at all times. Once you have reached this very strong level , this very unshakable level, then they know they have lost their battle with you. Then they can no longer touch you, but first you must reach this level. This takes concentration, discipline. and strength."

Christina said, "I am not so sure I am going to like this."

She tells me, "I am very much aware of it. But you see my little one, you are involved in this battle on both levels. On the spiritual level, for you are very close to us. And also on the physical level, for you are very close to those at that level also."

Christina said, "So I am kind of in between?"

She said, "Well, not really because you see, you are much stronger on the spiritual level than you are on the physical. You have already raised the vibrations of both bodies to such a level that you are much closer to the spiritual level and this will be to your advantage."

Christina said, "In other words I am like over half way."

She says, "If you want to call it that."

Christina said, "I am more strongly connected to the spiritual than I am to the physical. I have already achieved that.?"

She said, "Yes! But you are still very much connected to the physical body too, my child. This also is very important for without your physical body being in perfect balance and in perfect order, your spiritual cannot function

with the full capacity either. They both need to work
together and you know what I mean."

Christina said, "Sometimes I do and sometimes I don't."

She tells me, "Just follow your bliss, whatever. One
thought and we hear you. One wish and we will be with
you. We will merge with you. You will never, never walk
alone! That is a promise."

Christina said, "That gives me the strength."

She is saying, "Merging is very, very important on all
levels, not only with us. This will also give you the strength
that you will need. Your physical body must be nourished as
well as your spiritual.

"Until such a time when you have fulfilled your task,
and return to us, then you will no longer have to worry
about this physical body. Then you will resume your life as
an angel, living in the joy of the eternal presence."

Christina said, "I know it is important to understand, and
to hear all these messages, these warning signs. For we
don't know, and we probably would misinterpret everything,
and make it even worse.

"And I want to learn I want to be aware of it. I want to
know what to do, and how to help, and how to defend
myself. I feel that this is very important."

She tells me, "As long as you want to, we also want to
help. We can only help if someone from earth asks. And
when someone of your spiritual development asks, we can
and always will give our help.

"I feel a strong connection between two words, want
and need. It is not need, it is want! And as long as you
want on all levels, that is all you need!"

Christina said, "I see this red rose unfolding again. That
means that every time I come here, this red rose unfolds

which tells me that I have just maybe learned a little more. No I have raised myself a little bit more on all levels.

"Oh, I see this beautiful white blossom on top of my crown chakra. Its like a big white magnolia. What is the meaning of this?"

She tells me, "It is purity, it is strength, it is energy and it connects! You know what that means. The crown chakra has totally opened to the big white petals of the magnolia."

Christina said, "I somehow feel that I am very much honored."

And she tells me, "Yes, this is very special."

"Oh, I just don't feel that I deserve all this."

And she says, "Why not? It has nothing to do with what you feel in your physical that you are worthy or not. Forget the physical. It has to do with how well advanced you have become on the spiritual.

"It is only on the spiritual my child. That is the only level that can be of any interest. The physical body is not <u>our</u> main interest. That is <u>your</u> responsibility. You must look out for its needs. You must keep it in good health.

"Our interest is only with the spiritual. The spiritual directly connects with and guides the physical. The spiritual always comes first. And you, little one, must guide the physical through your connection with the spiritual. They work together, but first the spiritual, always.

"When we work with you, and together we keep your spiritual in total contact with us, you will find that keeping the physical in balance and in perfect health will be easy."

Christina said, "Oh, Mother, you say it so well."

"As she fades slowly in the shadows, her thoughts come ever so faintly, 'Of course.' Now to spread this message to all mankind."

We sat in silence as the graceful image of this special angel faded into the shadows. Every atom of my being danced in the sheer joy of her lingering presence. I wanted to remain in that eternal presence forever.

In light of the promise of an early return to this level of consciousness, the pathway back to normal consciousness became easier.

Meditation Lights the Way

We have just completed another ascension into the realm of the angels. From within the Temple of Knowledge, Mother Mary appeared in person before us, her dazzling golden aura surrounding us with rippling sensations of her powerful energy. I sat in quiet reverence before her, feeling her great mind reaching out and embracing Christina's mind and even extending outward to touch my own. The red rose in her hand sent its own message of love, as its subtle aroma suggested gardens of delight dotting the landscape of Eternity.

As pictures begin to flow gently from the angel's mind, Christina begins to speak.

She said, "Mother Mary is telling me that by coming and visiting her, we can lift our vibrational level very quickly to heights that are as yet unimaginable."

Mother Mary said, "You have been brought to these high levels so that when you are ready to remain here forever, you will know that its here, and won't even have to search for it. You need only to continue coming to this location, complete your development through contact with the angels, and learn to reach these heights with ease when the time comes for the final ascension."

Mother continues, "I am grateful for the help you have been giving your planet while in the whirlwind on your way up to this level. There is a little more light on the planet now, and it is beginning to help. But we need to attract others to help us execute the divine plan for healing your world and its inhabitants.

"All of your friends who work with you, are human souls.

They will be able to elevate themselves to higher and higher levels as they continue to help you to send more healing. The more energy and light that they send to the planet, the more that they raise their own vibrational level, and the higher they can develop.

"This is the reason that you need to tell as many people as you can, for this can be their way of also elevating their own consciousness to the higher levels. You must learn to raise your vibrations and awareness to the highest possible levels. For the higher your vibrations, the greater your ability to heal the planet and those who live upon it."

Christina said, "Even as you speak, I can feel my own vibrations lifting me to those higher levels. It's so helpful just to think about it."

She tells me, "The vibrations you then send out will be much stronger, and thus help the planet heal. Slowly and surely life on earth will become better, purer and much more meaningful!

"It will also create a healthier, and more spiritual atmosphere, where some of the souls there will be attracted by the higher vibration to those levels of awareness and of life."

Christina said, "You could say they will be magnetically attracted to these higher levels."

Mother Mary continued, "When the soul and the mind become strong enough within the spiritual body, the physical body will follow! The vibrational levels are magnetically attracted and connected to the universe, to everything on the higher levels.

"The vibrations work with your mind and soul and they are connected with your nervous system. Even connected with what you think, connected with your brain. This all works together. You have to begin with the vibration.

Everything else will follow.

"When you feel that you are uncomfortably trapped in a dense field of low vibrations, use the power of your mind and determination to lift yourself out of that area and back to the higher vibrational level. If your faith in yourself is strong enough, you can also raise those around you to this higher level. They will begin feeling the good energies of that location, and have no desire to return to the lower level.

"This is one way to become a highly evolved, stronger, purer human being. You will also fulfill one of God's plans for you. That is the reason meditation should be the absolute number one priority for everyone!

"Meditation brings with it a vibrational expansion. and a growth, that working together will lift you upwards into even higher and stronger vibrations. It will help you fulfill another of God's plans and His gift that goes with it. You can remain at this beautiful level as long as you continue to meditate regularly.

"This is the food for your minds, bodies and the soul. Meditation is also your vibrational connection to the heights of the universe. It is your strongest and only link unto these heights.

"It is helpful to use any form, but this is the masters' and angels' own meditation. In it you learn the cosmic whirlwind and how to attain the bridge to eternity.

"This bridge leads to your own special place of abode. Prudence would indicate the easiest and most practical path would be our own. Whatever form you use, concentrate on your soul level, on the purity of this total oneness!

"Those that meditate know that in order to climb unto the heights, this is the only way. You could never feel comfortable nor would you ever want to go to any lower level.

Your life will become a continuous expression of joy when lived surrounded by the sheer beauty and tranquillity of this, the ultimate experience.

"When you allow the angels' meditation to lift you to those levels of consciousness, you soon know that life without it would be unwholesome. That is, life without its high level vibrations and celestial contact would leave you with only the physical. Without the spiritual half found in the meditation, you would feel the loss of the missing part— contact with the spiritual.

"Meditation is the breakthrough to the higher vibrational levels. This is why this book will be so important and helpful to everyone, for it is the breakthrough made so easy for all of you. All you have to do is to step over to this higher level. Just step over!

"This book and others that may follow will be so very important. They will be important for so many people, but not for those that are on the lower vibrational level, because they have learned to live with their misery and any change to them they believe would be too painful.

"They do not want to experience more pain because they have existed in the lower levels for so long, it is easier for them to deal with it. What they will read will be painful for them in the sense that they know what this is about, but they really don't want to know. They will find it more convenient to remain where they are.

"This knowledge is the breakthrough that is needed to raise the life on your planet to a higher vibrational level. When that happens, you will become a better human race.

"Envision a fine-tuned, gem-like, super race that will be pure like a piece of crystal that glistens in the sun. Humanity will be like that crystal super race where nothing will be dull or hidden anymore. It will all be crystal clear.

"When this happens, the physical and spiritual bodies will come into perfect balance. The spiritual body will help to shield the physical from the evil forces of darkness that abound at the lower level. The spiritual will lead the physical into higher levels of vibrations and into an awareness of the unconditional love of God.

"Under the shield of that great love, and the power coming from the increasing high level of vibrations, the soul returns to a closer contact with the Creator from whence it came. With mind, body and soul in perfect balance, harmony reigns supreme. The exuberance of life in the midst of such peace and tranquillity, brings the full healing power of Creation to help make the already perfect being even more perfect.

"As you continue your association with the angels at these higher levels of awareness, you begin to see and experience them in their own environment. An overall understanding of their total existence takes form in your mind. Revelations of their special powers amaze you in the beginning. The scope of your total knowledge will almost overwhelm you.

"Bit by bit, you will learn the truth of your origin, your existence, and your lives. You will then know that much that has been written about you is myth that has been passed down through the ages.

"Most of all is the reason we have great concern and love for all of humanity. For within, you carry a soul which is a part of God. That soul is an angel, God's representative in this realm and on earth, imprisoned in a human body that is determined to deny even its existence.

"Yet that angel is assigned the duty of lifting another part of God's creation, the human body, into higher levels of awareness where it can develop its full potential. With its fully developed body functioning perfectly, the darkness that now surrounds you will be replaced by the brilliant light of God. Earth will then regain its rightful place in the interplanetary family of nations.

"If it fails, the angelic soul returns to God, and another imperfect body returns to the dust of the earth, from whence it came. If it succeeds, and once in a while it does, another body attains superman status, becomes a master, and then makes the ascension along with the angelic soul.

"As you continue this association with the angels, you will finally see the reason why almost every establishment on earth teaches us to blindly accept their policies. If you do, you will continue your total immersion in pursuing the pleasures of the physical. You can find it with little effort. It is all around you, everywhere you look."

As Mother Mary slowly moved off to the right, Christina said, "Good-bye, Mother. I love you. You know that I will continue to fulfill my promise."

Her reply came faintly, "The real path back to creation, with far greater benefits than the physical, remains difficult to find. The angels, with almost all of the power of the universe, must stand back and allow humanity to exercise its own free will. The untimely death of so many fellow human beings should be of great concern to everyone."

Still in deep meditation, Christina and I remained quietly in our seats. The revelations of the past hour filled our minds with concern. With so much information to ponder, the coming night could only bring a troubled sleep.

A Lesson For Earth.

In an intense meditation, Christina and I have spiritually arrived at our meeting location with the angels. They earlier promised a special session with valuable information of great importance to everyone on earth. As Christina began describing the location, she is saying, "I am moving across a meadow leading to a large building. I see the door open. We have learned the angels prefer to call it the Temple of Knowledge. It has balconies all around. The seats are a rich red color with a gold design around the back. The interior is of a tasteful decor. Many (angels) are here. They are all smiling and laughing with me. They are happy that I have come.

"Mother Mary is coming in. She is always barefoot. She wears a long flowing dark blue cape. I want to say, veil, whatever. She seems so happy to see us.

"Hello, my child," She tells me, "I share with you not only the love I have for you and for all mankind on your planet, but most of all, thank you for your faithfulness in coming here. Others have come but they lacked endurance. They continued with past involvement in earthly endeavors.

"Their greed and lust for power remained more important than spirituality. In other words they lacked faith. They were not strong enough to continue with any degree of dedication. They did not come back because material things were more important to them, and the desire for those possessions pulled them back down into the dark pool of negativity."

"This is why," she tells me, "the vibrational level is so important. It will protect you, and nothing can pull you back down again. Materiality can be a strong magnet, and there are people who can be led to fall back down into this earthly sea of madness!"

Christina continued. "She is evidently happy that I cannot be enticed to fall back down anymore. Well, I have to ask you something, Is it possible that I could be pulled back down into this darkness?"

And she tells me, "Of course. You have free will, but knowing what to expect down there, you will think about it several times, because you know how much you will be losing. This is why so many others have started out on a very high vibrational level and have fallen back down."

She is holding my hands telling me, "Feel my love."

Christina says, "Oh, what energy! Such beautiful energy. I know I am not saying this right. It is a love that just goes through my whole body. It is so overwhelming, so beautiful. This is the kind of unconditional love we do not have on our planet. I don't think we ever will."

Mother Mary said, "Yes. it can be achieved, but not until you raise your levels to much higher vibrations. Only then are you capable of sharing this love, of attaining this unconditional love. Then can you become these perfect spiritual human beings, living together in spiritual oneness, and not separated as you are now."

Christina said, "I guess that is what is so very important. We separate our spiritual body from the physical and one cannot work without the other. We have to become as one. We have to become fused together for one cannot exist without the other. Nothing will work. We have to use our spiritual body first, only then can our physical body function properly."

She is saying, "Spiritual nourishment comes first and that includes going within. Find this little inner peace, meditate, be in the silence, have beautiful thoughts, go to special locations that you feel good about. This is nourishment to the spiritual body.

"Only then can the physical body work, because then the physical body will be healthy, will be strong, will be functioning properly, will not do anything that goes below a certain level such as your negativity, your greed, your power, your jealousy. Once it falls to that lower level, you are right back where you started. That is the reason why you did not function well in the first place.

"So the spiritual body comes first, and filters down the energy and guidance to the physical. Only then can you function as that perfect oneness. They have to be fused together and this is how it should work between two people. Then they will work together in harmony. And their experiences and rewards will be perfect."

She tells me, "Its sad that the greater percentage only live at the lower level, so very far from the spiritual level. The gap is so wide, it cannot be bridged. This is why the human beings on the lower level find it difficult to raise their vibrations to the higher level, the spiritual.

"Their bodies are heavy, they are inundated with negativity and darkness and cannot lift themselves above it. They will perish unless they find this path, and the ability to raise themselves higher. Their physical bodies are dense. They are always sinking lower. Their souls cry to escape, but the body is too insensitive to hear."

And she tells me, "Because their souls are a part of God, the souls are crying to be free. And when the time is right, these souls will be free, because souls can never perish. Souls will continue to exist throughout eternity. A soul endures the physical body, always working to raise the body's level of purity to perfection. That is the reason it entered that body in the beginning of its life on earth."

Christina said, "I was once at that low level too, for she is telling me:"

"My child, you had to experience all that, but deep down at your soul level you always knew that this is not the level where you could be happy. Yet you were drowning yourself in negative things. In doing things that were harmful to your body you were trying to numb yourself. You knew then that this was not the answer to your problem. And every time you have fallen that low, you found the struggle harder to lift yourself out of that level again.

"You knew intuitively that there was a higher level filled with spiritual beings. This is where you really wanted to be. Yet when you were surrounded by negativity, you found yourself too weak to lift yourself back to a higher level.

"You were only dimly aware that we were always with you. We were there, ready to give you a helping hand. You were aware of this subconsciously. That is why when all physical energy was depleted, you reached for a higher energy level subconsciously, without being really aware. And that is why you now work so hard to learn the lessons that continue helping you move up still higher. You never gave up completely, because your deep inner connection to us was always there. And we are all so happy you have found and made the right choice.

"This began at your lowest level. The helping hand that we sent you was Ralph. He had to be there and gently guide you. Only with his help, patience and unconditional love, were you able to make it back to the level where you really belong. You are a very special child and have a special soul.

"And now that he has nourished you and strengthened

you, you must continue and complete all these other tasks that lie ahead of you on your own. You will and have become, very strong. We will always be there for you. I love you very much."

She tells me, "Faith is so important. Do not doubt yourself, but have the faith to accept everything the way it is. Don't let your thoughts dwell again of things that exist anywhere below this level. Allow your faith to become that strength you need in order to fulfill the tasks that are ahead of you—that you promised to do long ago."

Christina said, "As I think of that, all I can say is that it is a tall order."

She tells me. "Maybe from your side but we see it as a beautiful order, as something worthwhile because the end result will be what you will have accomplished.

"When you come back home you can look back. and you will feel so good with what you have accomplished. Your soul has certainly reached extremely high vibrational levels."

"And Mother," Christina asks, "does everybody have this chance?"

She tells me, "Of course! We would like nothing better than for everyone to come here, but that is only a wish and it will have to remain a wish for now. But we can help many, many that are looking to get to this level and don't know where to look. Therefore we will have to be this reaching hand to help and say:

"'Come, I will help you, I will show you, but I can only reach down to a certain level, and you must do the rest, merging your vibrational level.'

"For if they don't, they will have learned nothing and their bodies will remain on the lower level, and their souls will be sad. The Soul always hopes to take the body into higher levels. That is the reason it first entered the body.

"Without the physical body working with the spiritual, for the spiritual is always willing and ready to help, reaching this higher level cannot be achieved. Many do not even know that they have a soul—their own spiritual body. They do not know their inner selves. They are no more than strangers to each other. Most people do not look within, for if they did, they would find a total stranger, their own souls they didn't even know existed.

"They do not open this door to free this spirituality and work with the physical. They are living in separate worlds."

Christina said, "I don't believe I could find any part of this explanation anywhere else in the universe."

She tells me, "There is no time to read and search for explanations. Everyone should have this information now. If they knew and believed, all would join us in this effort. Working together, we could correct what is wrong and bring earth back to the Eden for which it was created."

"But there again," she is telling me, "time is running short!"

Christina said, "She is leaving us now."

We sat in silence, surrounded by the dazzling beauty of its colored lights, and the breathtaking energy of a reception hall filled with the presence of hundreds of light beings.

Yet, amid all this wonder, we missed the special glow that accompanied the presence of this great lady who had just departed our presence. Filled with the special glow of Her powerful aura and the power of her mind that had touched ours during the past half hour, our consciousness was lifted to unanticipated levels.

"Was it wrong to want it to continue?" I ask of no one in particular. Amid the flowing love from the minds of the angels, I detected a slight movement of Christina's head that could have indicated an answer. Was I wrong to think that as a result of our contact with the mind of Mother Mary, she had somehow detected my question.

A possible answer came from the movement of another angel upon the stage in front of us. Mataji, our own special master, and spiritual custodian of the Masters' and angels' Meditation, had come to us now.

Christina brightened from the power of her mind as Mataji stood before us in a stunning white robe, her glowing aura surrounding us with her love.

Christina said, "She is telling me that she is happy that I have finally made it to this level. She has been waiting for a long time. She has always been there for me but I wasn't aware of the full extent of her interest. She had worked through Ralph and he in turn worked through her for so long. They have worked to bring me to this level. And they continue to work together to help me, and many others reach these higher levels.

"Mataji and Ralph are a team, she on the spiritual and he on the physical. They continue to work with others, one of whom is Gregory. They are trying to lift him to the highest possible levels. He has advanced quickly, and is working quietly with us from a distance.

"Mataji is telling me in a very sincere way that what we are doing is the only way. The time is near, and for now there is no other way. We have no time to lose. It has to be accomplished or much will be lost. We have to become very serious about that and we could get it accomplished she said! Bottom line with Mataji is we'll do it!"

She is coming over and giving me a big hug and she said. "I know it. I love you. You're like a dear sister. Soon we will know that the Divine Plan is already in action and all we have to do now is follow our intuition and get to work.

"Just do it, don't question, don't worry, have your faith, have your love for all mankind, have your love for us and do it. Most of all have love for yourself. It is important to love yourself for if you have no love for yourself you cannot be this wholesome, giving kind of a person and therefore cannot show it to the others and cannot give it to others because you have emptiness inside of yourself.

"You must have the unconditional love and faith inside of you. It has to show. One has to feel it, one has to see it, one has to understand and when we reach this level to really show this and bring forth this love and faith. Then they know that we are real, that we really want to help from the bottom of our hearts. That is the only way. This will be our only credentials, our spiritual credentials."

As Mataji moved slowly to the back of the stage, and faded into the dimly lit background, Christina and I sat quietly amid the angels in the seats behind and alongside us. Christina will remain in the entranced state of spiritual contact for a long time, her mind savoring every precious moment of heavenly contact.

I feel the angels' love all around me. What a lovely feeling. What a totally content and fulfilled feeling. I am filled with the Eternal Presence of God. I know that I will slowly return to the world of our own reality. As of this moment, I am content, having one foot securely planted in each dimension.

What a wonderful feeling! Each of you are capable of doing the same.

Chapter VIII

Freeing The Soul

Today, they will show us much more about the developing contact between Christina and the angels. Note the growing friendship with them as they combine their general messages with special instructions to Christina. Interspersed within these messages will be much information about the true nature of their life in the angelic realm of existence, as well as on earth.

In this meditation, the angel Aliathor, liaison between the Crystal awareness and our own, has just allowed us to visit the dazzling beauty of the series of crystal caves behind large mountain ranges.

Christina said, "It is not easy to find this place. You have to ask Aliathor's permission to come. The energy is almost all that I can handle with comfort. They are telling me that there are many caves in this vicinity. Not just a few gems, not just gems, there are mountains of crystal. And every gem has a different energy, different power. That will be something for a later date, a study all by itself.

"They are telling me that there are many places here. You could not visit them all in one of your lifetimes. There is so much here to see. I am being told to just study and learn, one thing at a time. And really perfect it. And then go on to something else. Otherwise it will not penetrate and you cannot retain it. But it was magnificent and really beautiful, what he allowed me to see of it."

We have just entered the Temple of Knowledge. Christina said, "I am not sitting in the front row today. I am sitting in the middle. I am being told to sit in the middle. I don't know why. All of a sudden the entire front rows are just filled with masters, It might be a couple a hundred.

"And they are sitting with their backs toward me. I wonder what that means. All of these masters are just sitting there. But I see a beam of golden light emanating from these masters. It seems to beam upward. And it's like a big golden stand above their heads. It has to be their energy. It's unbelievable. They all seem to be waiting for someone, too. I can feel all of this energy right in my forehead. I wonder who they are waiting for.

"I see a tall, well-built master coming in. His shoulder-length. golden hair blends perfectly with his clear, loving blue eyes. Eyes that seem to penetrate the rows of masters ahead of me like glistening crystals.

"Quietness pervades the room. Everything is still. In the surrounding quietness, I can think of no one else to match his description, other than the master Jesus. It could not be anyone else.

"He looks like the Master Healer, but from the over-whelming power and love that surrounds his presence, everything about him suggests we are in the presence of Jesus. He stands tall and radiant, full of power and authority as he looks down upon the ascended masters assembled before him.

"Radiant energy flows out of his body and his hands. He seems to be only gazing into the group, his energy flowing down upon them. But I am now picking up mental sugges-tions of a soft spoken voice. Ideas like, 'I am happy you are all gathered here,' flow into my mind. 'The time has come that we unite more strongly. That we unite with everything on all levels. It has to become this oneness.'"

Christina said, "I still don't know what that means. He continues to gaze down upon everyone. I know they are receiving more information than I am. But that's all right.

These are special angels, the ascended masters. They are totally dedicated to the overall purpose of the divine plan they so willing work for.

"Now he is looking directly at me. He's telling me, 'You are included. We need to unite, above and below. We need to reach out and work together. Then you will know the meaning of this.'"

Christina said, "He's still standing there. His energy is just—I can't even describe it. He's just standing there, very still. And I know he's mentally communicating with these masters. It's just not for me to understand.

"And all of a sudden, he's moving to the rear of the stage. Something like a golden circle is following him. It's like a corona, that's right. And the next thing you know, all of these masters disappear off to both sides of the room.

"That was powerful. I'm almost speechless, All of that energy left me with a profound feeling of absolute awe. I can't even think of the word that will adequately describe it.

"I see this master coming back to the front again. And he is telling me simply, 'That was the <u>all</u>. That was the <u>all</u> <u>that is</u>.' Christina said, "I want to ask a question, was I supposed to be here. Was it a mistake?"

He just laughs at me and says, "Nothing happening here is ever a mistake."

"I guess I was supposed to witness that."

"He tells me that, nothing happens without a purpose."

And he's telling me, "This is a power not everyone is able to attain. This power is the purest of the pure. This is the creative energy of God."

Christina said. "I know it was a privilege for me to be here and witness it."

And he tells me, "There is a reason why you were

privileged to see it and to receive it. You will understand it better later."

Christina said, "That was really something. I have never experienced anything like it before."

Christina continues, "Now I see <u>Joshua and Tschen Li</u> coming. And I don't know if they were among the masters that were sitting in front of me or not. They seem to have this radiant glow around them. They must have been there. They never glow like that. And I like the smiles on the faces of both of them."

And they are telling me, "It is an honor to be in the presence of the <u>all</u>."

"And I don't know how or why, or even if I was supposed to be here."

And they tell me, "We will be the judge of that. This was a general meeting of the masters."

Christina said, "And I was present at one of those meetings. Is it some kind of a reward for my soul to have been in the presence of those masters?"

Receiving no answer, Christina continues, "And I guess that whatever my soul is doing that I am not really aware of, I must have been at an even higher level at that time than I thought."

And I just get this flash from Tschen Li, "We are aware of everything. We know everything, and we are very happy with the process, for you are keeping what you promised to do before you left us. It will not always be easy, for many will come and many will go. But do not worry about that. You just keep your eyes on that path, for you know the rewards are abundant. Soon you will know, my little one."

Christina said, "Joshua is not wearing a cape today, he is wearing a white robe, the same as with all of those white-robed masters. He definitely would not appear in his work clothes in front of the <u>all</u>. All I can say is, it felt like I was in the presence of God."

"Now I see <u>Mother Mary</u> coming in, and she's standing in between Joshua and Tschen Li. And they're looking at her with such love and adoration. They adore her. She must be their mother, she must be everyone's mother."

She's telling me, "My child this was a privilege for you to witness. Not many are invited to this gathering. So you see, I do not need to tell you that you have made great progress. So now you know."

Christina said, "And actually I'm doing so little."

She's telling me, "You're doing more than many of the others. You are reaching higher and higher. You are reaching out to many. You are helping many. You have a perfect human body surrounded by a spiritual body. And this is the way everyone should be. To know what you have to do on both levels, and to not ever step backwards. For we forgive all these little human mistakes, and we understand, and we allow."

And she's telling me, "You have helped your dear friend very much, the one that has just been with you. For she needed your support, and you helped. She is well enough on the path, but has to return to a very low level. And we understand. But because of your teaching and with your knowledge, you have strengthened her spirituality, and she will not fall back down to a lower level. And she will join you in due time, along with others.

"It is important that you are aware of all these happenings. For we all start out by accomplishing little things, and out of the little things come greater things, until it becomes so natural. And it doesn't matter any more how great we are. It's just a very natural thing do. For you have become so comfortable in that. For without this, your physical body could no longer function properly."

Christina said, "This is heavy. And she's telling me, "Your soul recognized this meeting. Your soul is highly developed. Your soul was very happy to be a part of this again. And all because you have progressed. You have given your soul its freedom so it can connect, and keep your promises. And this is what most are not even aware of. You are allowing your soul its freedom. Therefore, you will be able to understand more and more, as you give them the freedom to make these choices."

And she's telling me, "Soon you'll be able to attend more of these meetings, of these gatherings. And you will become very attached to these meetings."

Christina continues, "So it is like a gaining of more spiritual knowledge. That's why I want to and they're allowing me to develop my mind while I am still in this physical body. That is something not many are able to understand or to deal with."

She tells me, "But you have given your soul its total freedom, and you just follow along with your physical body.

Christina said, "And I guess this was the first time that I experienced what it means to give your soul this freedom. And then the soul can participate in all of these gatherings or meetings while it's still attached with this physical body. It is an honor."

She's just nodding her head. "It's more than an honor, it is togetherness on this level, on this highest level. Only a few are invited to these gatherings. This again was a spiritual growing meant for your soul only, for your development. Remember this well, for not all souls are able to receive and understand that."

"It is so easy, Mother. Everybody should come here."

And she is telling me, "Yes, it's easy, but most are not able to set their souls free, to let their souls wander, and to give the soul the freedom. Why not?"

She tells me, "They have not developed, they have not reached this high vibrational level. They don't even know it exists. And there's always this little bit of hesitancy there. But you have given total freedom to your soul. And others have not allowed this freedom to their souls. Like they reach a certain level and then they stop out of fear, but I don't want to use that word for it does not exist on our level.

"Because of not being able to reach higher, they do not have the energy, they do not have the vibrations, for the vibrations are energy to go as high as they want to. In other words, you have to learn to open yourself to all of this energy, to really be able to receive this energy. Without that, you cannot reach the higher level. In other words, you have to really open on all levels, and have the faith in us, of course. Have the faith in us. For your soul has the faith. But the soul cannot do it unless you cooperate. You have to set the soul free."

Christina said, "Oh, I see, like we are afraid the soul may not come back. It will stay up here."

And she tells me, "If you want to think this way, that's fine. But no soul will ever leave its body, until it is in divine order. And everything happens in divine order. There again, we must have faith."

She's handing me a red rose again. I always have this wonderful feeling, this peace, when I get this red rose.

And she's telling me, "This rose is also nourishment for

your soul level. Not only love and protection for you, but on the soul level, this rose is very important. It is like a support for the soul level, for the soul very much can relate to this. This is also love, and a soul cannot live without love. It cannot live without this purity. So that is like this food for the soul.

"You are picking up very well, my little one. It is getting easier for you to come up to these levels."

Christina said, "I understand in my very simple way."

And she says, "That is all there is, this simple way. There is no other way but simple. You must not think with your other body. Spirituality is simple. it's satisfying. it's harmony. It's all that there is. But all in simple terms.

Christina said, "Oh mother, it is so beautiful to have it explained like that."

She tells me, "We will be with you until you return back home. It was a special energy. It was a little gift for you. In time, you will know what this gift means."

Christina said, "She just smiled, a beautiful smile. The three of them are now walking to the rear. What a powerful message."

Christina and I slowly drifted back to our own world of reality. Experiencing beautiful dreams, we remained in the meditative silence of my study for a long time.

Chapter IX

Faith, a Magic Word

In an intense meditation, I sit quietly and listen to the voice of Christina as she speaks from within her own spiritual contact with that of Mother Mary, and often with some of the other angels attending us. From within these continuing contacts, many special words are repeated over and over again. Apart from their usual meaning, Christina's voice gives these words a special accentuation that bring them alive, and gives them a unique importance that approaches reverence.

My mind enjoys a special empathy with that of the angel. I mentally see the pictures and hear the words that flow from that powerful angelic mind. They reawaken in my own mind my promise to them long ago. Now, Christina is also promising to work with them until every soul on earth is made aware of the angels' love for humanity, and bring their message to the attention of earth's people.

Here you will continue to read of these contacts, and feel the manifest of their love in your own life. An enhanced understanding of the true nature of eternity becomes clearer and will excite you with its many possibilities.

And that brings us back to one of those special words—Faith. As our meditative contacts with the angels continue, understanding of its true importance brings the excitement of discovery into our lives. Properly understood, it becomes one of the most important words in this or any language.

Many times in the biblical story of his life, the Master Jesus used the word faith to account for his healing of the sick, and for some of the other miracles he performed. In many of those instances, he used the statement, "Thy faith hath made thee whole."

And in one of the Gospels he told his disciples that if they had enough faith, they could move mountains by simply telling them to do so. You might say that this is Jesus, the Christ, and it was possible for him to perform these miracles. However, he also told them that any one of them could do the same things that he did, and more.

The existence of the ascended masters and the story of their lives, tell us a little-known story. For once we are made aware they exist, and that anyone who finds the path to the light and follows that light to its ultimate destination, finds that they too can become one with that hallowed group. We find that the masters, those who have mastered their lives and learned the truth about existence, can perform the same so-called miracles when they finally understand that one simple word—*faith.*

Why did these masters choose to hide those powerful talents? There can be only one answer; the world was not yet ready. When I finally understood, I wondered if I would ever be ready. They showed me the number of philosophers of the past who had been put to death for possessing that knowledge. That made it easy for me to proceed slowly, and wait.

I later learned that the soul is there to guide the physical body in fulfilling its earthly purpose, that of continuing its upward evolution into purity, health and heavenly contact. Failure to fulfill that purpose will result in ultimate death and freeing the soul to repeat the experience again and again, until it finds a body willing to cooperate.

Another answer comes from the joyous welcome given us each time we make the meditative ascension to the angelic realm. Many angels greet us upon our arrival in the Temple of Knowledge. They treat us as honored guests.

Their energy embraces us, and prepares us for the special visits from other angels. They tell us that very few souls come into their midst while still attached to a physical body.

In today's meditation we find Christina visited by special angels, with messages filled with information concerning the special word—*faith.*

Christina said, "I see Jesus coming in now."

He is saying, "You have to allow everyone to express themselves as they think is right. Only then can they learn. Your soul can only become stronger when you give it the nourishment, the teaching, the freedom that it needs to develop for its own growth as well as that of the physical. Without this development, your soul cannot achieve what it needs to attain.

"Many are coming to this level, but only very few open themselves to this kind of meeting. because they do not allow their souls to become free, and strong. You have.

"I will always be with you. You know that, for I have great love for you. My mother and I are happy that we are now working together, and that I can help you in what you are doing. But you must make more of the effort. You must come here more often, for only then can you really become strong. For your soul has to wholly inundate your physical. Only then can your physical body become this wholesome, functioning body that your soul desperately needs.

"And you will have to complete much on your level. But it will become much easier when you come back home. For then, it will be only one thought away. And then you will remember everything."

Christina said, "I don't even dare to say what I want to say."

He's telling me, "No need to. I already know. Yes you are. You are every bit that what you think you are. Do not think with your physical, only with your strong spiritual mind. Only then can you accept the fact that you <u>have</u> attained your present level. Only then will you know of your self worth. Only then will you know how to respect yourself. I guess there will always be this little—he pauses for a moment, then repeats softly,—yes, this little doubt in you."

He says, "I understand. But you see, this is what we love about you. For you are always this straightforward person you have become on our level. And you are kind, caring and loving. And you are understanding. We need all of the above in order for you to complete the tasks that are before you. You have to achieve this happy oneness on both levels. All of this is important for your progress. Most of all, only than can life on your planet be that what you want it to be, that what it should be."

Christina said, "And I am getting this beam from his mind. It's like a laser beam, going directly into my mind, and becoming this oneness. And I am picking up this thought, Your mind is part of mine. And that laser beam just stays there. And I am picking up that I belong to a special spiritual movement toward the highest spiritual level."

"And yes," he says, "you can reach this level. But discipline is so important. Of course, you always have choices."

And he tells me, "I will always be there for you when-ever you need me."

Christina said, "I can hardly handle your power, your energy." He tells me, "You will in time. You always were very strong.

"He is now moving toward the back of the stage. His energy has lifted my vibrations a whole level higher. I know he came to take me as high as possible. I see Mataji coming out now."

She is telling me. "Now do you know what strength you have developed?" Christina said, "I don't want to say, I think I do. I want to say, yes I do. But it takes a bit of digesting first."

And she tells me very simply, "You can do it. I know you can do it. But you must learn to have this absolute faith. Your faith is still very weak. We have tried to show you what you can accomplish by faith alone. You must have this faith in everything that is coming to you. Only then can the divine plan execute. There is no doubt in the divine plan, there's only purity and clarity, and absolute discipline. And most of all—faith.

"You know that faith is so very, very important."

Christina said, "And sometimes I fail to understand the whole meaning behind faith."

And she's telling me, "Faith is everything. Faith is the absolute. In everything you do you must have faith.

"With this faith, you can reach out and meet the strength of your needs. This is how you attain the ability to raise your level, to open up more, to become more intuitive, to receive better."

Christina said, "I am now getting, "To connect better, that's a better word."

She said, "But then, remember, no matter what you hear or receive, if it is not totally clear, you know that your own faith will only let you receive that which is clear. And with your faith, you can move on, and nothing can stand in your way."

Christina said, "So many think they have faith, and I am seeing the word faith written in tiny letters. That's what they get, and it's not even legible. That's about how much faith they have."

She tells mw, "But you will also have the faith that all will be well on your planet. as well as having the faith that you will be protected, and you will survive. So you will have to help. For with that faith, there are many who will work with you.

"You can build mountains with your faith. You can move mountains with your faith. You can create mountains with your faith. You can lift mountains with your faith. So you see, you create another world with this little word."

And she tells me, "You are so strong. You can do it. I know what you can do."

Christina says, "I guess I will have to convince myself."

She smiles. "Whatever you want to do, if you have the faith, you can do it. Remember this. Just like you knew you could lead this meditation. For you do have the faith in yourself. Now that you have the faith, there is no more problem, there is no more doubt.

"Nothing is easy. You have to earn every bit of it. And no one can give it to you, or to work for you. You have to do it yourself.

"For no one is in possession of your soul but you. And this is the only way your soul can find that it can reach higher levels. Then your soul can become stronger. This is why everyone has the same responsibility for their own soul. No one can do it for them."

That's our problem. We think someone else can meditate for us. And she's telling me, "You know the truth."

Christina said, "And I am being shown a picture. It's a house with no windows. Oh, I see. Whether this house has Windows or not, it doesn't matter. Someone else can look out those windows, and see all kinds of pictures and views. But you won't believe it until you look out of those windows yourself. Only than can you know for sure what you see. Because it's your soul that sees, not any other soul. Only then can you know for sure."

She said, "This is why every soul must see it themselves, They must see, hear and learn themselves. No one can do it for you. Your soul will see the absolute truth.

"The absolute truth is, if your soul experiences and learns what it sees for itself and by itself, only then can you know the absolute truth. And no one can do it for you.

"So therefore, you must allow every one of these souls to express and learn and develop themselves. You can help, but they have to do it themselves.

"Everyone has to be given this choice and this freedom. There is no right or wrong, there's only one way."

Christina said, "How true, how true. And I am being told, These little lessons, these mega lessons are very important. Retain them, for only then will you have learned your lessons. By retaining them, applying them and using them."

She tells me, "If you only knew how much more you have to learn. If you only knew."

Christina said, "Maybe it's best I don't know."

She says, "This is why we are only giving you a few lessons at a time. So you can understand them well, if you learn them and if you apply them for our situation. Only then can you become this highly evolved soul. And others will know, and they will want to come to you and learn.

And we need many more just like you. For we need many to help."

"Thank you, Mataji. This has been a perfect session today. She's leaving me with this beautiful smile."

As she moves to the back of the stage and slowly fades from our view, Christina and I remain in this blissful state of awareness, every atom of our existence filled with the excitement and joy found only in this high level of contact.

We remain surrounded by other angels, whose presence enhance our own understanding and reverence. The special magic of today's lesson on <u>faith</u> touched us deeply. We will remain in the lingering presence of the angels' message as long as we can, and finally carry it in our hearts long after we return to our own world of reality.

Chapter X

Mother Mary's Rose, A Symbol

Christina said, "I am sitting in my special seat, on the front row, at the Temple of Knowledge. I once again see this beautiful red rose on the arm-rest of my chair. As I touch it, its magical aura surrounds me with an overwhelming aroma that carries me into a delightful state of euphoria.

"I see <u>Tschen Li</u> and <u>Mataji</u> coming."

Tschen Li is saying. "When you share this information with others, there will be many who will eagerly listen to the messages you bring from the angels. They will be anxious to cooperate when they share your experiences, and see for themselves the revelations the angels bring.

"With our help, you can bring our message to many more people. This is how you can spread the angels' messages. This is how our healing energy can be taken to every one on the planet. People must be clearly informed of this work, and that it must be done daily.

"They should never stop bringing our healing to the planet, and they should reach out unto others. You need to start this chain reaction, in fact a domino effect all over the planet. This healing will in turn come back to you with the added help of the Angels and Masters. People must make the effort to realize just how important this is.

"For this is but the beginning. There is so much more beyond this that you will have to do. We hope you can reverse an uncaring attitude most people have for your home—your own planet earth. They have little concern for their abandoned waste that slowly poisons its atmosphere and surface.

"They will have to learn that the opposite is true. Earth is gloriously alive. It lives its own life, with every function in perfect harmony with the natural laws of the universe. Only in this meditation can they align their own lives in harmony with these same natural laws."

Christina said, "In this meditation, we are with the angels in the Temple of Knowledge. We see, feel, and understand that harmony. We can also see and feel the miracle of the planet's life flowing within and around us. A planet that speaks to us in the life-giving wonderment of its natural functions.

"When compared to life on earth, most of us live for whatever physical pleasures we can find, and neglect the spiritual body—the soul, that is patiently waiting for our contact."

Tschen Li says, "I will be there for anyone who needs my help. I will always be there! The time has come for everyone to work together. You will need this oneness, with the physical and spiritual working together. Then you can become strong enough to overcome the darkness that is slowly destroying the life-giving energy that once moved so plentifully over the face of your world.

"We are at the point where this is very, very serious. The darkness here is far worse than anyone really cares to realize, and only the healing and the light can keep these negative forces from destroying the life that remains. These forces have no power over the light and healing."

Christina said, "I see Joshua coming in, and he is telling me to share this message with the sword, so that others will know of its extreme importance. I am being shown a picture of them healing the planet, and visualizing the sword spinning counterclockwise around the planet. The forces of darkness cannot exist in its presence."

He is saying, "Absolutely nothing can touch the symbol

of the sword. People are to visualize the sword going counter-clockwise around the planet, and this needs to be done with love and kindness. There is never any darkness around the sword for then it cannot be effective. Only with kindness and love can this sword be used. The angels will do the rest."

Christina said, "Joshua is showing me the sword with a big rose embedded in the handle. This rose is the symbol of love, purity, strength and power."

He says, "Some progress has been made, but more will be needed. The darkness knows that more of you are drawn toward the light. You need the energy of many more people working with you. With their energy added to your own, the combined energy will help overcome the forces of darkness.

"While we need much more assistance, I am grateful for that you have already given. For with everyone working together, its total accumulation will make a difference."

Christina said, "Mataji is now telling me that love and kindness must prevail. It cannot be any other way. Never forger to let love and kindness intertwine with everything else. Without that, there is no balance or harmony.

"I now see these Masters standing behind each other. Joshua is first, then Mataji followed by Tschen Li. They are all merging together, and all I see now is that big, glorious sword and nothing else.

"They are showing it to me as a symbol of power, purity and love. They used their special ability and merged into this sword because it represents power. This sword is glowing yellow and gold, and that is their purity and love injected into this sword.

Mataji is saying, "This is love as it is supposed to work.

You are to merge yourselves with this sword as we are now doing. Then you will become this power, strength, purity and love, that is so desperately needed on your planet.

"This is why you are to see the sword encircling the planet in a whirlwind rotation, and at the same time knowing that you are that sword. This is how it is to be explained. You can all become this sword.

"You are these little swords which can also be equated to the spirit world where you are these little soldiers helping the big soldier, which is Joshua. Our little swords equate to the big sword."

Christina said, "I am being told that it doesn't matter who is doing this inner work, as long as we are all doing it together. There is no one individual. There is no one person doing this alone. There is no one better than the other. We here are all equal, all the same for we are all working for the same cause.

"There has to be equality, for every one is accepted as equal. Only then can we make the difference together in love, balance and harmony. In the Masters' world there is only equality, for nothing else is measured, for all souls are the same. There is no higher or lower, there is only the one love, and it is that of equality."

Christina exclaims, "I now see Mother Mary coming in on a beautiful ray of sunshine. Her robe of brilliant white glows as brightly as the sunlight illuminating her dazzling smile."

She tells me, "You must know why it is important to raise your vibrational level. You need to do that so you can clearly receive my messages and my thoughts. As you raise your vibrational level you will become purer and more aware, then you will not miss any of my thought forms.

"These are the great rewards that you will receive when you raise your vibrational levels. These rewards are so overwhelming that they cannot be compared with anything else.

"You are to continue bringing everyone you can into the higher levels of the meditation. Not only for all of its powerful benefits to their health and spirituality, but for its ability to bring them to this level with its contact with the angelic realm.

"Tell everyone who wants to come and see me, that I will be there for everyone. In order to share my love, you are to present each student with a rose. It will represent my strength and love for everyone.

"Many people do not know how to share their love with me, or how to ask for my love. This rose will be the connection, and many of them will be able to open their awareness to a higher level.

"Many of them could become my teachers of the truth. The teachers of these heavenly truths will be the connecting link with Creation that everyone desperately needs. You who teach must always mention my rose.

"Teachers must become the joining link to the many, and for this they must become not only very strong within, but absolutely sure through their purity. Only then will they be able to reach out and become this strong link.

"These teachers will become the magnet that many will want to become attached to, until they become ready to attain that level on their own. To those who become teachers and work with you, please remember that they will never have to teach alone. The Masters will always be there to help and guide them.

"With this knowledge and through the inner connection in Mother Mary, we will be able to help many others. This will make a difference to everyone who seeks a solution to life's many problems.

"As each of them takes this inner path, they find that it will raise their vibrational levels to heights they never dreamed possible. So many of them are desperate to find the true solution, and would dearly love to grow. Yet Mother Mary is telling me, "We must be careful. There are always the deceitful ones. These are not even aware that they are inundated by those at the lower vibrational levels."

"My teachers here must be able to really listen well for only then can they detect these lower levels, these lower shadows, for they would so much want to tear you down and devour you so, Be Very Careful.

"This will become part of the learning experience and we all must become aware of it. Mother cannot do this for you. You need to become totally immune from all these insidious powers at large in your world, and you must also know that it will become worse. These powers will want to discredit you and tear you down. So you must always be aware.

"It is like a ship on the high seas in a very thick fog. Even though you cannot see, you must be aware intuitively that there is another ship coming, and there will always be danger of a collision. You cannot see it, but you can feel it intuitively.

"This is where you will have to become strong and alert, because you will not be able to see it. However, you will intuitively feel it with your increased vibrations. In fact, you will soon develop the ability to pick up everything. The higher your vibrations, the more intuitive you will become."

Mother tells me, "As others get stronger, they will be able to help still others to become stronger. You are part of my spiritual family on your planet, and will be the link to many all over the globe. They are all my children and I love them dearly. Since I cannot reach that many, you will have to help with this book."

Mother is sending me this wave of love, and telling me, "This is my love for you to become even stronger so you can share this love with everyone else."

Christina said, "I wish I were a little bigger, then I could handle this better, Mother."

Mother said, "It has nothing to do with size, it has to do with the vibrational level. Only then can you become strong enough to receive all this love without losing some of it."

Christina said, "Mother tells me that she is pleased I made the choice to communicate with her in meditation. For I have made many wrong choices in life, but she knew that I would make the right choice in this instance. When I felt Mother's vibrations, my soul knew what it wanted to do.

"Mother was right there trying to help me make the right choice, because she had more of a connection with my inner self than I had at the time. I told Mother that she was able to make the connection because of who she is. And she said, 'I had a little bit more experience.'"

Mother tells me, "I want you to accept me as real as you can, and to know me as best you can in whatever way you want to express it. That will help us become closer. That will make it the reality you want it to be and I do want it to be. Only then can we accept and connect on all levels."

Christina said, "Well, you couldn't get any more real, Mother. I feel you, I hear you and sometimes I see you. I know you. The only thing that is lacking is reality, and reality is there, too.

She tells me that, "It pleases me that you understand so

well, for not many can understand. Many think I am this
being, for lack of a better word, in outer space. This being
way up there, unreachable and untouchable, but I am not. I
am very real. I want to be on everybody's level that is
acceptable.

"I am very much this mother that wants to love her
children, but there is a certain level of purity and respect
involved. Only then can I reach out directly and touch them.
They must raise their vibrational levels as you have. That
must come first. Without the increased vibrational levels,
the connection cannot be made."

"In other words, Mother, the gap is too big and the
signal is too weak.."

And Mother said, "I am happy that you can accept it and
express it so well, but I am very real."

"I think it is just because we humans think they want to
touch you for the reality sake."

Mother replied, "You can touch me, but only in spirit,
for I am not in the flesh.:

Christina said, "I am thankful that I can reach you in the
spiritual."

Mother Mary said, "Yes, I can be reached, but only in
the spirit, and that can only be done through higher
vibrations. For vibrations are energy, which is spirit, which
is everything. That is why vibrations are important. They
are the key to your inner world, and also to the angelic
realm. And the key to contact with me and all the other
angels."

Christina said, "They are the key to everything. Even
my physical body is affected by them. That is why it seems
so warm in here. They have raised the temperature of my
body. I think the more I understand this, the more my own

vibrations increase. And as I feel them within me, they are expressed in me as energy, and react as heat in my physical body.

Mother is laughing and saying, "It can react and affect you in many ways.

Christina said, "Well, I think this special meeting was the most, I want to say, down to earth conversation. I feel that I don't even know how to express myself."

She says, "You are doing just fine. Express it on your own level, in your flesh body, the best way it is for you to understand. It is for you to know in the spirit body exactly what I am trying to convey to you."

Mother Mary says, "The higher the vibrations that you can attain, the more often I will be there with you and the more real that I can become. Working together with me, you will attain the ability to mend broken hearts. You will learn to erase many emotional problems, and heal many people. Doing this is what the Masters' and angels' Meditation is all about.

"You must open to all these connections, for everything is in the Divine Plan. Most human beings do not even have knowledge of the Divine Plan, or how everything is connected to the Divine Plan as well as the Divine Order."

Christina said, "From that look, Mother, I get that this is where we come in, to help as many understand as possible. Whoever thought that I could have such a lovely, I want to say, relationship with you."

Mother replied, "We have always had such a wonderful relationship."

Christina said, "Mother is reaching down with her rose and touching mine, so that it just opens its petals, and, Oh, what beauty. Her rose melts into mine, and it becomes one big unfolding rose. And she is telling me, 'I am sharing my rose with you.'"

Christina said, "Mother is leaving now, and smiling and smiling."

As the Great Lady moves gracefully into the dim light at the right of the stage, she slowly fades from view. The many angels seated around us continue to sit in the stillness left by her departure.

Christina and I remain in our seats, still in an intense state of higher consciousness. The movement back too our easy chairs at home is only a slight drifting sensation, and into the realization that the intense energy of the Angelic Realm has followed us. We will remain in the consciousness of the Creative Mind while the lingering sensations of ecstasy and spirituality remain with us.

As a by-product of the verbatim conversations between the angels and Christina, you will learn much about that realm of existence. I know of no other source from which these truths can be learned. Read it carefully, for this is where your soul will dwell through eternity.

Only truth can flow from the minds and hearts of angels and masters.

Faith, Mastership and a Warning

The important lesson on Faith continues. That one word previously filled me with sensations of love and beauty. As these meetings continue, it now fills me with awesome implications of power, hidden abilities, and little understood accomplishments. It lights the pathway, opens the doors to the hidden by-paths and detours, and leads the faithful across the once hidden bridge to eternity.

Even after one walks amid the intriguing wonders of the angelic realm, reposes in the rapture found only in its fertile orchards, gardens and vineyards, and shares the eternal presence of God with the angels. Faith will perform awesome magical wonders that continue to surprise and delight.

Read the many references to faith in the following meditative contact with Mother Mary and the angels. The Archangel Raphael begins the contact as he instructs Christina in the work she has agreed to perform. He speaks of faith and truth as he tells her how to bring these truths to those she is now teaching.

Be aware that much of what he has to say is directed to instructions for her use alone. But as you read the account, everything he tells her is tremendously important to the life and survival of everyone on earth. It is presented so that everyone can learn these truths and apply them to their own advancement.

Many people are searching for answers they can use to change their lives. Know that what you hear from the lips of angels are lessons in reality, and truths that can set you free. The same is true for the other angels that teach Christina in this meditation and all of the others. Herein you will find, in the angels' own words, the most powerful revelations of the nature of eternity and what it means to humankind in its harried existence on planet earth. The solutions it provide will work in the lives of everyone who seek answers to their problems.

Continuing this session, Tschen Li, my one time earthly teacher, substantiates the information given by Raphael. After that, he gives a stirring account of the catastrophic events that could befall our planet if mankind continues to use it as a dumping ground for his destructive waste and a repository for his careless thoughts.

Then Mother Mary comes in grace, beauty and love. The tender moments she shares with Christina should fill the hearts of many with longing to share similar moments with this great lady or one of the powerful angels that work with us.

Just remember what we have said several times before. Mother Mary and the others have promised to work with any sincere person who will come to them in the same way and manner that we do. Even now, Christina and I are both teaching others to do the same.

This session begins as do all others. We have just arrived meditatively into the angelic realm, on a special planet. Christina continues, telling of our approach to the Temple of Knowledge, our usual meeting place with the angels.

Christina said, "I am approaching the big building which is the temple. They (the angels) are waiting for me. The doors are wide open. There are not too many here today maybe twenty or thirty and I am picking up that they are more advanced souls. Some of them, of course, are not as advanced as others, and these are the more advanced.

"They are greeting me with a melodious sound, that sends its soothing rapture to fill me with its welcome. They always sing in perfect harmony. A special energy fills the temple with love, and most of all welcome. So many beautiful combinations of sensations greet me. Everything is special; the air, the aroma, the melody, the love, a combination of so many things. It is such a great honor just to be here. I am grateful that I am permitted to come.

"Even the air in the temple is special, nothing like I usually have to endure on earth although I live on a mountain where the air is purer. I feel joy as each breath easily fills my lungs with rich and living oxygen. This and other special ingredients send their special energy and power through my bloodstream and into every cell and atom of my body. It is almost overpowering. The rich energy is about all I can handle in one breath.

"I am seated in the front row. As usual, there is a beautiful deep red rose waiting for me in my chair. It is only a bud, but a special one that never has any thorns. Its aroma is out of this world.

It is dark in here. Just a little light on the stage, but it is peaceful and quiet. I have Raphael coming. He seems to be seven feet tall. He tells me, "Welcome my little girl, we have been waiting for you. It is very important that you came today. You will know the reason during the course of the day. For now, just prepare.

"This is part of your learning experience, a part of your continued spiritual growth that you are learning here. You must learn to adapt. You must learn to accept without question for only then can you strive towards higher elevations or higher levels, for there are no mistakes here. This is part of the Divine Plan, and it must be followed in the

Divine order. There is only one way. If this way is not obeyed, it will fail."

"Does this mean for everyone individually," Christina asked, "or for all humanity or, both?"

Raphael said, "It is for all. Many have the wrong concept of what will happen for there are many false teachings, many false prophets. Most of humanity has no faith, for if they did, they would go within and connect with all of us and all that there is and they would receive nothing but the truth.

"This is why it is so important that souls like you and others will come here to receive nothing but the clearest and the most precise truth of all. Faith is so very important and a complete and perfect faith that most of humanity cannot ever understand.

"That is why they remain at such a low level when, if they followed the same path that you have found, they could remove the mountains of darkness from around them. By developing a simple faith, they could move into the light and reclaim their true heritage, the one their ancestors lost so long ago."

"But," he tells me, "you have made progress, little one. Your faith is overcoming many problems for you no longer question, you no longer analyze but just follow your faith. And everyone should follow this pattern.

"I know you have been sharing this message with others but they perceive it only as mere words. You have to learn to penetrate. You cannot use, I want to say, softness or kindness, or maybe they don't want to accept. You are to explain it in a very loving but yet precise method for only then will they know the real meaning of faith.

"Only then will they become aware of the reality and the

importance of faith. If they do not have enough faith, how can they have the faith in our messages? In that event, the plan cannot and will not work.

"So whatever message you receive, whatever feelings you receive, have faith, Braid it into these messages. Then can you follow this straight path, this direct path. Only then will you know what is to come."

He tells me, "There will be much cleansing on your planet. Most of the need for the cleansing, or its resulting upheaval, results from humanity's neglect by man himself. And most of it in the name of control and power.

"You must be very careful for the controllers are very insidious. Share this message with those that want to hear and want to learn. For that control is like a fatal disease, hovering over humanity and robbing it of everything, including its own life.

"Always consult your spiritual body first before you express it through your physical body. Your spiritual body is aware of all knowledge around you, good or bad and it alone will protect you, and always want to protect you. Remember this my little one, for it is this part of a learning experience that we have to go through."

He tells me, "This is all part in growing and learning and accepting the faith, faith in its entirety, the faith in the all, in the everything there is. This faith will be your tool for protection. This faith will be your strongest tool, so you can see how important it is for you to grow and surround yourself with this faith. There again, this is also protection."

"I understand," Christina said. "I am having this funny feeling like something is running down my forehead. It is like something is running inside of my forehead. It is like a tingling sensation. And he is just looking at me."

"Just have the faith and accept." he said. "Do not always question."

"Thank you," Christina said, as he walked slowly back into the shadows. "Now I see <u>Tschen Li</u> coming," she continued. "He is wearing his dark suit again."

He tells me, "It is important that you listen to these messages from someone else other than me. For all of us have different vibrations. Some vibrations are more penetrating than others. This is why more and more will be included in these learning experiences that you are going through."

Christina continues, "And he is telling me how happy he is with my progress and because of this progress that I am making I am becoming stronger and stronger and everyone will pick it up and know that I have changed. The change had to come from the inside in order to show from the outside."

He is saying, "Most people can only see what shows on the outside. The inner glow is beyond their ability to perceive. They see the special glow these high vibrations radiate on the outside, and perhaps feel the vibrations if they come near. As the angels continue to teach you, the increasing vibrations surrounding you will bring more of them to you."

And he tells me, "Most of them are very inquisitive, and you are giving the right answers. You are telling them that you have made this commitment towards spirituality for the remaining time of your existence on your planet. Many will be there to support you and help you. Many will work with you.

"There will be a great cleansing, for much of it has already died and it is slowly falling off. I am seeing trees that are just falling down because of lack of oxygen and nourishment. I am seeing mountains crumbling because of various acids and poisons and toxins around them.

"I am seeing rivers drying up because due to the lack of rain, and I am seeing fields dying and drying up. I am seeing many cattle and animals dying in the fields. I am seeing many humans dying and that tells me that there will be a great drought for that is only one part of your planet.

"On the other part I see many floods with houses floating down rivers, animals floating down, humans floating down, cars floating down. And on another part I see volcanic eruptions where there is smoking hot lava flowing everywhere. It is smothering the land and covering almost everything.

"But scattered here and there you can see little safe and dry areas. This is where you will find small groups of people who have found a measure of security from the disasters.

"They are led to these safe areas because they heard our call back to Creation from people like you. These special souls responded, and are preparing to join with our effort to recreate and rebuild earth into a better and more perfect spiritual planet after great changes have taken place."

And he tells me, "You are one of them. And you will have the help of the like-minded. There will be little groups like this everywhere. You will become enlightened to a degree that you can make mental connect with them.

"You will know approximately where these groups of people are and you will be able to send mental messages across. This is how you will communicate and you will gain information and knowledge and for that you need faith."

Christina said, "And I am seeing the word spelled faith like a hundred feet tall."

And he tells me, "This is the only way I can tell you how important it is to have faith. I am trying to give you the best analogy you can understand in this . . ."

Christina said, "I know what you want to say, you want to say primitive body."

He is just smiling, he says, "How well you can read me. You must discipline and purify your body even more for only then will you be able to use your mental capacity to make these contacts. You are already using your mental capacity."

Christina said, "I want to say predicting but that is wrong but I can't think of anything else. Oh, predicting some of the answers before you even speak them, you know, or before you have proof."

He is saying, "This is already a part of development for you will know what will happen somewhere in the near future. You are not always precisely right but it is a beginning because the faith will allow you to know exactly what and where it will happen and how it will happen and what you can do to help and improve this ability is to fully use your <u>faith.</u> Perfection will result from acquiring higher vibrational levels."

And he tells me, "You have the strength the purity and the faith within you, but you cannot find them or feel them until you clear away some of the clutter, garbage,"

He just laughs at me, he says, "That's what it is, because of all these many years you have been informed and taught wrongly and believed wrongly. For only after the cleansing will everything work out. Only then can everything become perfect on all levels."

Christina said, "I know you looked and saw all of this happening, Tschen Li, I know."

He tells me, "You see, your faith and your vibrations are already picking up my meaning, does this not tell you something?"

"I would say so."

He said, "This information you must share with others that want to learn, that want to grow, that want to accept and then want to help. Do not waste your time with others for you have no time.

"This group that you have is a beginning and they will all learn and have the faith and will graduate and will go on and form their own groups. This is how we can reach out but they must be very selective."

Christina said, "I understand!"

He is leaving now. I see Mataji only in the background

I feel <u>Mother Mary</u> coming in. There is just a little hint of sweet air, with a kind of a gentle breeze in the air. Oh, there she is. "Oh, Mother, it is so wonderful to see you."

She says, "My beloved child, you are radiating the love and the spirituality you have become, and I am happy for this is the beginning. You will gradually have more understanding and tolerance towards everything that you will encounter. This is the beginning of the leaning towards mastery!"

Christina said, "Oh, that is heavy.

And she tells me, "No, and you are well aware of that. Your mastery existed before you came into this body. This is not a new word for you, for you have mastered many things before.

"Your soul is very much aware of it but it cannot do anything without the support of your physical body. Your soul knows what it has to do and what it can do and what it should do. But it has to have the support of the physical body, otherwise there would be no need for a physical body. From where you are on the physical plane, you cannot exist just on the spiritual realm alone. You must exist on the physical plane. Purity, discipline, faith, all are tools for you to help this dense physical body to become a lighter body. Then you will be able to connect and flow with the spiritual body at all times on all levels.

"Towards the end you will attain your mastery. Then you will have kept your promise and you can walk across that bridge at will. Then you will have become one of the masters. Only as you finally walk across this bridge to eternity will you have your reward."

Christina said, "You know, Mother, if many more would hear these things I think they would do anything to fulfill that which they have promised. Then they would all eventually want to become like that."

She tells me, "They all want to, but the flesh is weak. They do not want to give up anything physical. They do not give their spiritual body the permission to grow and expand. The spiritual body is totally suppressed within the physical. Only once in a while the spiritual is able to attain a free moment.

"You have permitted your spiritual body to become strong, to become greater than your physical. You have given it the freedom to find its way back to Creation. In so doing, it continues to take your physical body into ever higher levels of attainment."

Christina said, "Maybe only once in a while I kind of forgot."

She tells me, "That is very normal and we understand and we accept. But you have allowed your spiritual body to become strong and pure, and want to allow it to grow greater than the physical. And you want to remember it at all times. You don't just remember it occasionally."

She tells me, "Like 24 hours a day? No, we look at it as the eternal now. There is no 24 hours a day, or past, or future. We have only the present and you have to learn to live in the present and let us guide you through the eternal present for that is all there is.'

"Christina said, "I get not just the passage of time, but that the present is all. Which means there will never be an ending. All will only be the ever-present."

She tells me, "You have raised your vibrational level to a point where I can discuss this with you and you will understand. It will take a little of your time to digest. But the main thing is that you know what I am trying to explain to you.

"You already pick up very well, because as I am speaking to you it already resonates within you and it resonates back out through me and it resonates back through you. This is how it has to resonate when you are with someone else for if this does not echo back and through you, be very careful.

"This is where faith comes in, in yourself and in us. I know you have your son visiting with you and he will do well for he is also guided very closely. He has been given another chance. Had he not turned towards the spirituality, towards the right path he would not be anymore! He was given a second chance and he chose the right path and he is very much aware of it.

"He will be supporting you very much on many levels and you will know when the time is right. He will equally have a spiritual partner and he will be happy for he is also a special child."

"Thank you Mother, that is comforting to know. Thank you so much. I know I shouldn't say thank you but I feel so inadequate."

She tells me, "I am here because I know that you want to learn and to know that you have become strong enough is all that we need,"

Out of nowhere she is bringing her rose and touching mine and it is becoming this one huge unfolding rose with the sweetest aroma. She is pinning the white ribbon on my left shoulder again.

Christina said, "I know Mother, I haven't forgotten."

And she tells me, "I am happy you shared this message with others for this is a little seed that can grow if they allow it to. This can be the beginning of the purity on all levels. Some will remember. That is all you can do, Everyone is responsible for their own spiritual growth.

"There can be no power and no control. There can be no forcing, only a gentle kind of caring and guiding. The rest is up to everyone. They must want it. This is the learning experience. Everyone has to want to. It is their responsibility. Only then can they become what they have promised to be."

Christina said, "I understand. She is leaving now."

As Mother Mary fades into the darkened part of the stage, Christina and I sit in quiet contemplation amid the cherished memories the angels have given us. One day we will gather the courage to tell the world the wonders these magic moments have brought into our lives.

This is a special spiritual contact with the angels. I hope you enjoy and cherish every moment as we do.

Other Magic Words

We have arrived in the Temple of Knowledge and
Christina is speaking. "We have the <u>Master Healer</u> coming.
He's stretching his arms out, and he says, "I am happy you
are here. How I wish we could have more like you. But in
due time I know you will bring more."
He tells me. "This is why it is important to reach out to
as many as we can, before it is too late. For many are
searching, and still unsure of how and who to contact. And
many have been hurt. They are cautious. They fear being
hurt again."
He tells me, "As you become stronger and stronger, and
others are joining you in these efforts, fewer will be able to
harm you, especially the beings of darkness. Because of
them, you have to become stronger. That is why you need
the faith, for it can and will help you."
And he tells me, "You know that I will do all that I can
to help. But we will also need your help. When you ask us,
we will be at your side all the way.
"You are to work for the goodness of mankind. With
your pure heart and close connection with us, you will be
totally guided. And to those who are not aware of the
danger, you are to tell them in a gentle, loving way."
And he's telling me, "Have faith for you have made a
good beginning. For spirituality must prevail in your plans,
and nothing can harm you. This is the only way."
Christina said, "It's like the last plea they made to us.
Many have been directed to come here. When they come,
we will join together and work for the ultimate good of all. .
"But we must have the faith. And we must pass it on,
for that is the main purpose Ralph has been working for so

long with such patience."

Christina continues. "Now I see <u>Tschen Li and Joshua</u> coming. He (Tschen Li) has on his dark suit, and Joshua has on his red and golden cape. They're of big stature. Who wouldn't have respect for these two! The way they stand up there like—'don't even think of anything.' I get the thought that you will be dealt with before you even think.

"And <u>Tschen Li</u> is telling me, "I am working closely with all of you. I am traveling or roaming your planet. I am picking up much sadness, much darkness, much pain, much sorrow, Many are hurt through no fault of their own, just for the sake of power and greed, and control!

"I am feeling, not only for the souls, but also for the physical body. Because it also has feelings, and suffers the consequences. They are victims of the circumstances. And they are not even given a place or a standing in your world. They are under total control."

And he tells me, "There is so much pain that they are without a thought of healing the planet or of helping mankind. It will be of some help to the soul level, but not to the physical. But that is only flesh and bone, the frame that has to carry the soul. Your thoughts are being picked up on the soul level, bringing much needed nourishment and encouragement to that level. To a small degree, the soul won't be totally alone in the physical body.

"And that is why you need to do this to help the soul. It's not so much the physical body that needs our help, because they do have doctors to help. But for the soul, there is no one there. And that is why you have to be there to help the spirit.

"That is why it is important to send healing and energy, and use the symbol of the little sword to keep the negativity away. And use mother's red rose to send love. For that is the only help the soul will be able to receive.

"That's why it's important. The physical body can get help, but the spiritual body is the angels' concern. And that's why they are pleading with you. We need to send help to the spiritual, to these many imprisoned souls. And they are in prison because of mankind's greed.

"The souls didn't agree to come here to be in prison. They agreed to help the body grow and become pure, and to learn, and to be healed. But they cannot do it without the help of the physical body.

"So the spiritual body is blameless. That is why you need to help."

Christina said, "That makes sense. Now I know, and I will explain it to others."

Joshua says, "Now you know why we urgently need your help. For without being asked, we alone have no right to interfere. Now you see why we have to stand aside and allow everyone to make their own decisions. But with you on the planet, wanting to help your own kind, only then can we support and reach out and help.

"We can help you because you have asked. We will help you get others to help you heal. We will help any of them when they ask. Only then can we support and reach out and help."

Christina continues, "In other words, we have to help our own on this planet. You can only help the spiritual body because you cannot interfere. The divine plan limits your helping the physical unless they ask.

He is telling me, "In other words, the soul, while in the human body, will always strive to lead the body into spiritual contact. Over the centuries, human greed has grown so strong that it finds desires of the flesh more appealing than the spiritual love of God. The soul must endure the wayward direction the body has taken, but working always to awaken that body to knowledge of the path back to creation."

Christina said, "Now I can see. Now I know. For we have free will. And you have to obey universal law, and cannot interfere, no more than we can interfere with the universal law without suffering the consequences. And as long as we follow the path of greed, power and lust, we must pay the consequences And the ultimate consequences is pain and death. All of this need not be if we but find the path back to creation as was originally intended.

"Thank goodness that some of us have found the path. And we are now using our time and talents to show others the way."

"Now I have a question for you. It's only a little one."

He says, "My little one, I am well aware of your question. Where is your faith? Wait and see."

"I guess I had that coming." He tells me, "You will never learn if you don't have the faith. If you don't have absolute faith, it cannot work."

They are walking to the rear of the stage. Now I hear this lovely music, and I know that's <u>Mother.</u> She's on her way in. She is accompanied by increasing vibrations, the sound of music, and a delightful aroma. Ah, there she is. Her smile radiates such unconditional and overwhelming love, with the sound of music, and a delightful aroma. It is so overwhelming I find it difficult to accommodate it all."

She tells me, "You are receiving all this much better already. You really need this love and this energy. Just remember this one little word—<u>faith.</u> With it, everything will and can be accomplished. In other words, faith is equally as strong as the word love. For faith can become a vibrational feeling of accomplishment, of balance, of harmony.

"Faith has a very strong vibration. The word is only a mere word, but if you listen to its vibrations, that is what will bring you all of the accomplishment you need. Just use this word *faith* over and over again, and put your feelings into this word, then you will receive the vibrations that make it work.

"Just like the word *love.* If you express it in a very loving and sincerely committed way, you will also pick up the vibrations of the word love. It all has to do with the way you feel it and the way you express it. That is vibration. Just as music is vibration. Just as *poetry* is vibration. All this can feed your vibrations. This is why it is important to surround yourself with these special powerful aids leading you back to God. That is how you can grow, and help your soul reach those higher vibrational levels. *Faith* and *love,* what powerful vibrations, all leading us back to all there is."

And she tells me, "And when you combine these two words, feel the vibrations of both of them working together and giving you the ability to literally *move mountains,* or accomplish any other worthy deed. It's as easy as that, once you understand."

And I am being told, "This is why it is so important to come here so I can teach you. So all of us can teach you. Another important vibration is simplicity. It has the simple meaning of, 'no problem, I can handle it. I can deal with it. I can accept that. I can make time for that.' That's the vibration of the word simplicity."

"This is why," she is telling me, "you must choose your vibrations in your expressions, in your tonality. They are also vibrations that are being picked up by others. And these are key words, keys to work with, tools to work with. How to express yourself, the tonality is what breeds life into your vibrations.

"And these vibrations will resonate in others. And from this will come your own confidence. This is where you will awaken the attention of others in what you are teaching, first on the human level. Then as they grasp the full intensity of what you are teaching, it will awaken them on the soul level.

"They can raise their own vibrations into ever higher levels of the soul. Finally back to the human level and help them conquer the frailties of that level. Only then can the soul level become as strong as it needs to be to lead others back to Creation and salvation."

She is telling me, "Mankind is in dire need of this vibration. Never lower your vibrations by using the wrong tonality, the wrong sound. If not, you will lower your own vibrations to the level of others. If you do that, they will be able to pull your own vibrations down even lower. Never give them your permission to do that."

Christina said, "Oh, I see."

She tells me, "Always stay on the highest vibrational level. Only then can you continue to help. Only then can you remain strong. And never put yourself in a position to be pulled down by someone else. Never give someone else the power to pull you down."

"Thank you mother, this is all so simple the way you put it."

She says, "I love all of my children, regardless. For we have unconditional love. If we didn't, all would be lost."

"In other words, you can overlook and forgive all of the horrible things they are doing to themselves in following the path of greed, lust and control?"

She tells me, "I only see the soul level. Nothing else. For nothing else matters. For the soul is a part of God, a part of all of us. I hear them from the point of unconditional love, from the spiritual level. And there, nothing else exists but the soul."

Christina said, "And I am seeing the white figures of all these beings or other angels floating all around us. And she looks at them with so much love."

And she says, "This is how all mothers should look at their children. With this unconditional love. If a mother cannot express love for a child on the physical level, how can they ever express it on the spiritual? They must raise their vibrations and advance to this level in order to do that. This is why I have to be the mother for all."

Christina said, "I can feel that we don't deserve this."

She tells me, "It is not a matter of deserving. The spiritual body deserves it all, for it is without fault. For the spiritual body is a part of God. Think not on the human level, shift your thoughts to hearing on the spiritual level."

And she tells me, "Make this a part of your learning experience."

Christina said, "There is so much to learn, and it is so simple the way she explains it. But I know it will be difficult to explain it to others." A deep sigh comes from Christina.

She tells me, "Just keep on as you are doing now. There will always be those who will follow you and come up to these levels with you. And those are the few we have chosen. And they will work with you. Keep the faith, my little one. And remember that faith is powerful, it is the magic word."

"Thank you, Mother."

In the magic of that beautiful moment, I sat in my chair,

filled with the intensity and rapture of the unconditional love of God. A love that filled my body with ecstasy and radiated lovingly through the room and beyond to whatever physical range He and the angels wished it to reach.

We had just completed nearly an hour of spiritual contact with the angels, yet remained in continued contact with each of them that had spoken, and all of the others that surrounded us here in the sanctum sanctorum the angels called the Temple of Knowledge.

What a wonderful, simple message. If only more could join us in learning and teaching these messages, we could change the world for the better, and perhaps avoid the terrible consequences we are creating for ourselves.

Christina sat quietly at my side, still in the intensity of the spiritual contact we had just made with the angels. In the timelessness of that special location, we could remain as we were, still in contact with the angels, for whatever length of time we wished, even an eternity. In this location, there were no limits.

We now knew that our souls were angels from this high level. For varying parts of our lifetimes on earth, those souls had been voluntarily imprisoned in our physical bodies, allowing those bodies complete control as we thought only of the transit joys of that lower level.

We became free when we allowed our souls the freedom to return to their home for brief periods of R and R. They always take us with them on these frequent vacations. Now that we know the complete story, we know these powerful spiritual beings would never abandon us, but would remain with us as long as there was life. After that, we could rejoin them in everlasting life.

The Life Force Energy

It may be difficult to visualize a relationship between the spiritual Life force Energy and the scientific principle of relativity, but it does exist.

On the physical plane, matter manifests in its various forms according to the rate of its vibrations. And at the high end of the scale, atoms vibrating at that level became Light.

Similar results are manifest on the spiritual plane as well, but they are known not as Theory but as the Natural Laws of the Universe. Violation of those laws carry an inescapable penalty often called karma or karmic consequence. If this violation continues, the natural consequence is called death of the physical.

On the spiritual plane, there is no such consequence as with the physical, for no one attaining that level would even think of such a violation. The natural consequence of this positive behavior carries its own reward. The masters and angels refer to it as Everlasting Life.

The meditation we practice to make contact possible with the angelic realm is called the Masters' or Angels' Meditation. We use it to make spiritual ascension into the highest levels of awareness and attain contact with the masters and angels. This process makes a powerful addition to anyone's life.

One of its most powerful benefits comes from attaining the ability to create large quantities of the Universal Life Force Energy at will. At that level, one feels the obligation to share that energy with mankind. The joy that comes from sharing brings with it the joyful assistance of the angels as they accompany you on your journey to enlightenment.

The above explanation is necessary to this chapter, since

Mother Mary and other angels are speaking to Christina on the subject of vibrations, and healing and other benefits from the use of the meditation's Universal Life Force Energy.

To assist you in understanding the part Christina plays in this chapter, remember she has been a student of this method for over a dozen years. She has mastered and is teaching both the meditation and the healing that goes with it.

You will note in the following contact Christina and I make with the angels, that the angels, especially Mother Mary, instruct her in many phases of the use of spiritual vibrations and the Universal Life Force Energy.

In this beautiful meditation, we have just arrived in the angelic realm, and have completed a brief period of enjoyment amid the picturesque surroundings of this special place. We are now approaching the Temple of Knowledge, our usual meeting place with the angels.

Christina is speaking. "I hear the sound of music from the temple. The time has come for me to move gently across the lake and the meadows, and into the open door of the Temple of Knowledge. The angels welcome me with their own special choral music, so beautiful, so melodic. The vocal harmony thrills my inner self into a joyful awakening into the fullness of soft, gentle melody.

"And I am receiving a gracious welcome from the light beings assembled to greet me.. Actually they are angelic souls, and they are floating around me, below, above, and beside me. They are welcoming me through their vibrations, telling me how they missed me. I am slowly floating onto my chair and there is already a rose lying there. There is a light beaming down from above, falling upon the floor of the stage in front of me. That is it, I don't see anything else.

"Now I can see <u>Tschen Li</u> emerging from the semi-darkness behind the light. So tall you can't miss him, he reaches out to me with both extended arms."

He tells me. "I am happy to see you again, even though we are together many times, but only for brief moments. It seems that I always have something to tell you, but here is where I can give you more than just a brief message, I can teach and also lecture you."

He says, "What I have to tell you today is very important. It is about a special energy the angels call the universal life force energy.

"This energy is present and available for everyone. When you teach it, it has to be presented, and explained in the right manner, very methodically."

He tells me, "The universal energy is there for everyone but very few are aware of it and don't know what to do with it. Therefore it is important to teach it properly. You have to explain how to apply it. And, most of all, the symbols that enhance it have to be taught correctly.

"What you call attunements are not referred to by that name. We refer to them as the uniting of the symbols with the physical and spiritual body. In their coming together in perfect harmony, through contact of your level with our level, the physical and mental contact you make can be called attuning.

"We cannot do it alone. It has to be done through the contact you make in total purity, balance and harmony. Only then can the energy flow freely and this is what is important. If this is not done properly it cannot work, for if we did not attune, we could not be connected without this contact there!

"And this is where Ralph has been a very strong contact between us and your planet and now my child you will have

to learn to become another contact. You will have to work
and become much stronger. You will have to learn and
study. You will have to know everything, otherwise it
cannot work if it is not applied or taught in purity and
knowledge.

"Only then can you see results. Only then can you have
this healing effect. You will have others to help you but you
will have to become very strong and raise your vibrational
levels even more to become this pure contact, this pure
channel between this energy of the universe and humanity.

"In other words this connection between you and the
human body is what is important, for it has to be pure, it has
to be in touch with the universe as well as the energy and the
Masters.

"It cannot be taught or given by just a word or a symbol
for then you will have nothing. And you see my child, you
will become a very good teacher for you have done this
before. First your soul level must become stronger. It can
only work when you have reached a strong vibrational soul
level."

Christina said, "Then it is the soul level that I once was,
that I need to work myself back up to?"

He tells me, "Precisely. Your soul is not as strong as it
used to be or as it was in other lifetimes. For you have not
always nourished your soul level and now you have to
continue your present effort to reach that very high soul
level again.

"Only then can you be the best teacher that you need to
be. And others will know that your teaching is special. They
will know that your energy is special for they will experience
the results. You do not have to convince them for they will
find out themselves. Your work will speak for itself."

He tells me, "The healing will become extremely important very soon. The balance and harmony will no longer prevail on your planet. There will be levels of disharmony and imbalance, more than you care to see or hear.

"You will know when you are in your own space. There you will use this balance and harmony and energy. When you do, nothing can touch you, nothing can get you out of balance.

"You are not yet fully aware of the power of this energy. This is why it is important for you to become even stronger to reach this higher soul level in order for you to produce this energy in its purest form and strength."

Christina said, "In other words I have to work a little bit harder."

"Nothing is easy," he tells me. "You have to earn the name teacher! Only then will you be worthy of our teaching and able to work with our energy."

Christina said, "In other words I need to reach a stronger and higher level. Then I am worthy to teach this energy of the universe that you would approve of."

He tells me, "Yes. And they will know by your deeds and you will be known by your energy.

"Purity, strength, and energy is what is involved, nothing more, nothing less! We have been giving you the information that this is very important that you need to know everything. You cannot hesitate, you have to know everything. Only then can you represent this universal energy. Only then can you be this contact that is worthy on our level.

"But so far you have done what you were told to do and you have done well with your teaching and you have made progress. They all understand you and what you are trying to explain.

"But your teaching must become stronger. Your changing world will have more and more need for this energy and this healing. It must become simple, clear and pure. And it must be available for everyone who is sincere and who will use it. Do not waste your time on the others. Time is becoming short,"

Christina said, "I get this message that you are sad because of the wrong teachings, because of the energy others are wasting trying to teach something else that is not really energy."

"It is actually nothing," he tells me. "It is just the greed and the power they are seeking. How can energy possibly flow when there is nothing but greed involved? There are no rewards for these teachers, none whatsoever!"

He tells me, "I know what you can do, and yes, you have to do much more. This will enable you to become the good teacher that you have been before. We know you will become a great teacher!"

He continues, "The main thing is that you understand and know what I am trying to tell you. Also, you know and understand when I tell you, you <u>are</u> a great teacher. Your soul will recognize that, and that is all that is important!"

"He is now walking away to the rear.

"I see <u>Mataji</u> coming. With only a brief smile as a greeting, she begins where Tschen Li left off.

She says, "Yes it is of great importance that you know of the purity and the strength of this energy. It has been abused for a long time. This has to be stopped! It must no longer be abused.

"They will know that your teaching is of the purest, of the strongest energy. And you will get your rewards when you conduct your next seminar, for you will see and your students will tell you of their progress because they are applying the principles in their purity. They are sincere. They are very much aware of how well it has worked for them and I know that this alone will give you the energy to reach even higher levels.

"Nothing comes easy. You have to earn everything. Only then can you be worthy of being who you should be. Time is of the essence. Time is very important and it is important that you teach this seminar. They will need to learn more in order to help their own people. No part of this planet will be exempt. The heartache, and pain, and suffering will be everywhere.

"This is why it is important to use the Life Force Energy. Without it, nothing could survive on your plane. Access to it comes from dedication and acceptance. It is freely taught by the angels who wait at higher levels and work with all you and other teachers bring with you to that level.

"It can only be attained in its purest form from the purest teaching. Then it will work. And they know you are a good teacher. They know it comes from the spirit level as well as the human level."

She also tells me, "Nothing will be without rewards whether they are on the spiritual level, or on the lower level. For everyone gets their rewards. It is not easy to follow this path, but if you continue to follow it, you will reach the level that is of the highest and purest energy."

"Then you can be the best teacher, the one that you have promised to be. You will also have help. You will always have help, and they must be of the equal purest teaching. Then it can work.

"As you teach, you will know who among your students will be the purest teacher. You will always know. You will always know who will be true to you and who will not.

"It will become easier and easier for you. Your energy and vibrational levels are becoming stronger and stronger. Increasing intuition will be your reward, because you will be able to tune in more and more, and you will know without a doubt who is of pure thought and deed and who is not.

"Just go within and you will know. Do not let anything stand in your way. You must continue this path upward. You cannot look back for you must look to the present, always to the present. Only then can everything work."

She tells me, "I am so proud of you for you have made great progress."

Christina said, "Just think, I could have done it a long time ago if I had only tried."

She tells me. "This is not important. Do not look back, look to the present.   We are all very pleased with your progress. Of course, you had the best teacher."

Christina said, "How well I know.

"She is leaving, sending me her love, just so much love.

"Mother Mary is coming in. She is carrying a big red rose. She is nodding to me."

She says, "I have missed you my child, but I have been watching you and I am always very happy when you are thinking about me and when you are making contact with me."

She tells me, "The vibrational level that the energy is on is a combination of both of them.   In other words, the vibration and the Life Force Energy are together. They are one. That is why in order for you to become the best teacher that you can be, and with the purest energy, you have to raise your vibrational level.

"The higher your vibrational level, the stronger the life

force energy will become. They work together. This is why you have to try to raise your vibrations higher and higher. The higher you go the more of the energy you will be able to combine with the vibrations.

"Everything is energy and vibration and everything is vibration and energy. When they are merged together into one force, they will work together to make your life perfect.

"Those that are on a low vibrational level will have low energy and those that are on a high vibration will have high energy. You see how important it is to work even harder, to become this strong vibrational energy and oneness."

"Vibration and energy is vibrational energy," Christina said. "How easy, I never put these two together."

She tells me, "Everything is connected, everything! You see my little one as long as you stay connected with every-thing there is, you cannot ever fall, you cannot ever do any-thing wrong. But if you are disconnected, nothing will work. The vibrational energy is part of the Divine Plan.

"So this Universal Life Force Energy that you are teaching, is directly connected with the vibrations, with the Divine Plan, with everything."

Christina asked, "Why haven't you told me this before, why didn't Tschen Li tell me that before?"

She is smiling, "Because everything is being explained at the right time. Now that you going on your trip you need to be aware of this energy and be able to use it. That will make you the very strong teacher that you can be, and that you will be now that you have the knowledge.

"In order for you to reach this higher vibrational level, your first requirement is this meditation. With it you can go within, find your own inner strength, your own inner purity, your own inner balance, and thinking only positive thoughts.

"There you will find unconditional love, kindness, helping one another, understanding, caring, rising above trivial thoughts and deeds, connecting with the All, everything that there is.

"All of that is important on the spirit level. However, there is your physical level. You cannot raise the vibrations within and without your physical body unless it becomes purer. It must become less dense, much lighter. In other words, it must work to become purer, to free itself of excessive toxins and harmful materials that clutter and impair its normal functions.

"Do not overload your body with extra weight, with wrong foods, all this is part of having a lighter physical body that everyone needs.

"And you have begun this therapy, this new life style, and that has already helped. You are purifying your physical body and we are very pleased for it can then follow the spirit body easier and better. It can connect on higher levels. All that will help to reach a higher vibrational energy."

"So what I am doing is right."

She tells me, "Yes, but don't stop now. There is much more to do, and much further to go. It will make an even greater difference, for you will bridge the gap even more after you purify more."

Christina said, "I have the feeling this has to do even with longevity."

She tells me, "It has to do with everything. Everything that is connected with your physical body, your spiritual body and everything that is connected out there. And yet everything is really very simple. We just have to make a little bit of an effort.

"Yes my little one, this is all that is required, a little

effort, very simple! As you increase your energy, and raise your vibrational level, you will increase the electro-magnetic fields or the electricity around and within your body. This will help raise your physical body to higher levels and will re-energize everything within the electrical field around your body. It will be a, **rejuvenating, re-energizing, and** regrouping."

And I am being told, "All of that and more. That is together with the Life Energy, with the vibrations, with a less dense body, but a stronger vibrational level, with a higher advanced soul level spirit body.

"In other words all this will help to raise density, electro-magnetic fields, cellular structures, health wise, everything!"

"Oh Mother, it is simple and easy, but it takes discipline, it takes work."

She said, "Nothing is easy, nothing is free. Everything has to be earned, only then can this be accepted within the Divine Plan. It will not accept anything impure or anything dense. For Denseness results out of the lower vibrations. Denseness is matter at low vibrations. Light results from attaining the highest possible levels of vibrations."

She is just telling me, "You see my little one, all this should have never been lost. All this should have been practiced from the very beginning.

"I must tell you, mankind has fallen from what it was first intended to be and to do. They have become so weak in their will to maintain the soul level that they had at first, when life on this planet began."

Christina asked, "So now why are we being taught at this late time of our existence on our planet? Why couldn't we have been taught this 20 or 30 or hundreds of years ago?"

She says, "Then you would never have learned all of your lessons. This was the other reason why your souls came into this life to learn other lessons, to know what they can and cannot do from within the human body.

"First, let us consider that mankind always has free choice. We have found that the right choices are not always made. Even now, I know that many who are on the path cannot make the right choices because of their heavy dense bodies and their mental conditioning from childhood.

"Their brains are filled with clutter. Combine that with the weight of their pollution-laden bodies, you find they cannot contact the soul level or the spirit body, and this is the big problem.

"They are not making enough of an effort, they are not making the commitment. Without commitment and discipline, they are unwilling to remain on the path even for a little while. Then they fall back into their old habits and all is lost.

"You cannot do that. It has to be a daily discipline. You cannot ever stop."

Christina said, " I have a feeling this message was strictly for me because of what I have to do and what I have not done."

And she tells me, "Yes, it is for you now. But it is also for others that you have to teach later. But first you must be learning these lessons yourself. Then can you become the best teacher that you can be, that you should be, and that you will be."

Christina said, "I get this feeling of being told like a good teacher always has to first do his or her homework before they can teach this subject to someone else!"

She tells me, "Your intuition has improved. We have told you many times before of our great concern for the deplorable state of affairs on your planet. Whenever we finally work through one area of negativity, and feel that within our limitations we have it under control, another one emerges to take its place."

"It seems that the same thing has been going on from the beginning of the history we know of our planet, "Christina said, "perhaps even before that. Will it ever change?"

Mother Mary said, "Not when the physical desires are a substitute for spiritual contact. In fact, it continues to grow worse."

"Will it ever stabilize or improve?" Christina asked.

"It hasn't in two millennia that I know of," she replied. "Even with the assistance of the many other angels now helping us, we are not making the progress we hoped for."

"I am doing all I can," Christina said. "Tell me what else I can do."

"Just finish my book as soon as you can," she replied, "We will help you put it before the public. If enough of them believe, and help us the way you have, we still have a small chance of turning it around."

"If we don't make it?

"We will never stop trying."

"I can feel your concern," Christina said. "Can you tell me more about it now?"

She tells me, "Not today. We are having a meeting at another time. First you must digest all you have been given. Only then can you be ready for your next lesson."

The aroma of delicate roses fill the air, along with the soft gentle music of Mother Mary's song as she departs.

As she fades from my vision. I felt an inner emptiness of the magic of her presence. The vibration of her love remained and filled the gap left by her departure.

Other angels remained with us almost constantly. She had promised to come whenever we were ready. Relaxing in my easy chair, I slipped slowly back into the loving arms of this wonderful vibration. As usual, Mataji and Mirva came to reinforce the message I received today, and I knew what I had to do from here to eternity.

A Different View

When the angels permit me to see each scene depicting the message they send us, I wish every reader could feel the intensity of the love and concern for us that flows freely with it. With time, the dreamlike reality of each session gives way to vivid actualities. You are there. You can see, feel, hear, and live the beauty of each scene they bring you.

For I am also present, as a witness who shares each word, scene, and exciting revelation as it flows from the angels into the finely attuned mind of Christina.

Each of these meditative sessions becomes another spiritual contact, similar to entering into a deep state of prayer. Inspiring sensations accompany the high levels of contact. and trickle down into your inner being. Awareness of entering another dimension of time and space flow in and out of you, bringing with them feelings of joy and bliss.

Fatigue and stress fade into nothingness, replaced by a surging flow of inner healing, relaxation and energy. Meditation is taking you into a level of spiritual contact you never before thought possible.

There you somehow just simply know which decision to make or which path to take. Everything is within easy reach, if you want to learn or change. When you find your inner self, you bring your life into a balance that makes you a part of the solution and no longer the problem.

The main problem, and its possible solution, becomes the most often repeated concern of the angels. It is frequently repeated by one or more of them in almost every session we have. They tell us that the problem can be avoided if we can reach enough people who are willing to help. In helping us, they also help themselves to a more satisfactory earthly existence while adding their energy to a possible solution. Quite often, these different meditative contacts with one of the angels contain powerful information, for this book. I repeat it almost verbatim. Consider that Christina is in meditation as she speaks, and in total contact with the angel who brings the message, and can clearly present its meaning to us.

In meditation, we have made the journey from earth in our spiritual visit to this planet. Christina and I are now ready to enter the Temple of Knowledge.

Christina is speaking, "I already had a wonderful experience on my way up. They have given me energy and love, healing, balance, and harmony. They have energized every cell in my body. I am being told that I will need this in the future for what I promised to fulfill.

"They are preparing me to achieve total balance and harmony within, and to become almost totally fearless with the inner strength one receives up here. I think that alone is a wonderful gift and I am very grateful,

"And they tell me that this is for everyone who wants to come and who wants to learn. It is for everyone, not just for a few, for there is more than enough room for everyone on our planet.

"I am walking through the door and into the temple. All around me, everything is very still. Seated in the room are many light beings (angels). They are quiet. They are not moving around today. It is a different pattern from other times. It feels like everyone is expecting something special, waiting for something to happen.

"It's like being seated in a concert hall, feeling the magic shortly before the concert begins A hush settles over the room. Everyone is full of anticipation. No one even dares to breathe deeply. This is the kind of feeling I get.

"I am now sitting down. A feeling of anxiety has inundated my being. I don't know whether I should be excited or not. I have my two Masters behind me and I feel their hands resting on my shoulders. They comfort and reassure me. Of course, it is always a powerful experience.

"Here comes Tschen Li again. It seems that he gets taller every time I see him. He is wearing his dark suit."

He tells me, "Welcome my little one. I can see that you made much progress. From your teaching, many are beginning to send healing to the planet, and we are seeing the results.

"Your message has helped, for it is spreading. You see, this is only the beginning of what you have to do. When you go on your trip, you will also have to spread this message. Many of your friends are also eager to do their part.

"It is very important that you continue to share all you have learned so far. Do not forget. This is also part of the plan. They will listen to you because they love and respect you, and know that you are speaking from the heart. In our case, it would be the soul."

"He is showing me very quickly all the destruction we have had since the beginning of the year and this is but a fraction of what is to come. And I don't even get a time. They don't tell me the time, it is not important. Just prepare on all levels.

"It is going to be a part of the cleansing and the healing process. It can only begin by first burning out, I want to say, the cancer that continues infesting our planet, and with it humanity and all living things. That is what will happen unless it is destroyed, and every bit of toxicity is eradicated. Then we can allow life to begin anew.

"I almost want to compare it to chemotherapy, and he tells me, well, not quite like that. I get the feeling that he doesn't like the word or association with that deadly process and he tells me no! But in order for our planet to heal, this will have to take place and this is the only way that the planet can regenerate.

"I am getting that this is a bad thing for humanity, but it has to take place first before the planet can heal and regenerate and become this healthy, loving, beautiful, kind of planet that it was meant to be from the beginning. But mankind's failure to seek pure spiritual contact, and unconditional love for all even from the very beginning, has finally brought this condition into being."

He tells me. "I am proud of you for you are fulfilling what you have promised. Only a few have given even a single thought to fulfilling the promise they made as each soul joined a body for the duration of life on planet earth. Finally a few are consistent in their commitment and now that you have started, many more have followed suit for they see the changes in you."

He tells me, "I don't have to convince you, you are being told on many occasions. That is at least the proof that humanity needs to change its direction. Everyone has neglected finding their true spiritual selves for so long, now they have too little faith in themselves. You are learning to grow in your faith and with that comes inner strength. Of course you have a lot of support in becoming even stronger and believing in yourself and us.

"I am so very happy that you have finally started to fulfill your commitment, for this is the reason why you are here. This is the reason why Ralph returned, as well as many others that you are not aware of, but you all had free will and choices and we are happy you have made the right choice. We only offer our unconditional help and you have received and listened well."

Christina asked, "Why couldn't some of the others receive this unconditional love as well and know which way to go?"

He tells me, "Because everyone is on their own level of development where their style of life and selfish interests have put them.

"We do not interfere. For the spiritual body has to be in harmony and connection with the physical body. They both have to work together or development and growth cannot occur.

"So you see, little one, spirituality has to be the strongest body for only then can it help the physical. If the physical body is stronger than the spiritual, then nothing will work."

Christina said, "I am seeing this dark heavy dense toxic body just being weighed down. I am being shown if you put a very heavy Christmas ornament on a branch that is very weak, it bends the branch and is hanging all the way down harming and spoiling the appearance of the tree. A very light ornament will remain level with the twig, resulting in an attractive tree.

"So that is how our body should be, very light, so it would be in balance with our spiritual body."

He tells me, "I have special love for all. You are all very dear to me! I will always be there for you and with you as well as all the others. Right now you are under my special guidance. Of course this is also in conjunction with the Divine Plan for everything works through and with the Divine Plan.

"Most of humanity is not aware of what the Divine Plan

portrays, what it stands for. You must speak out and you must explain. Once they work within the Divine Plan, within the universal law, they know unequivocally that life will work and life will become better on all levels."

Christina said, "Well, Tschen Li, since you are walking the face of our planet, maybe you can walk . . ."

He is smiling at me and saying, "I know what you are going to ask me. I <u>can</u> walk into the area of the planet you live on. Just wait and see."

Christina said, "How very cautious of you."

He tells me, "You are always the same. You will never change. How well I know you."

Christina said, "He is walking off to the right."

"Now I see <u>Joshua</u> coming in very briefly," Christina said. "He is wearing his red, golden cape and I can actually see a glow coming out from under his cape and I know the reason why, because his sword is hanging from his right side. You would think it would burn a hole in his cape but it just glows through it. It is kind of a light green and golden glow and he is marching very swiftly across the stage and looking at me briefly. I get a fleeting thought like keep up the good work or something like that.

"Now I hear the soft sound of harp music mingled with the sweet aroma of a rose garden. It is telling me that <u>Mother Mary</u> is about to enter! Here she comes now, walking gracefully across the stage in front of me.

"She always comes in and sits down but I never see a chair. It is strange that I never noticed that until just now. A small golden globe floats under her feet. Everything is perfect and normal and I guess I took it for normal so I never noticed it before.

"She is passing me a rose again. I tell her, 'I know this

is your love for me. Thank you Mother.' She is also passing out roses to the others that are sitting in front with me."

She tells me, "I am pleased with your work, and to know that you remain committed to your promise. That brings me much joy. Others have now joined in this commitment.

"I think that you will soon hear about it, for some of them now feel that this is the final purpose in their lives. They know it is more than the other everyday earthly commitments, for this is a spiritual commitment. It satisfies a special need within their spiritual selves. It is something that they have been searching for so long, and it is easy for them to do.

"It only takes a little of their time and effort. But they always get some benefits out of it by reaping the rewards of feeling better of being more harmonious and balanced, of losing the fear they used to have of exercising more courage. It is just an overall good feeling for which no pill or drug on your planet could ever substitute.

"This is a natural well being. a natural high. Some have already noticed that their spirituality has grown and become much deeper and more rewarding on many levels. It is so simple. Everyone has been chasing so many different things that came their way and nothing or little has ever helped."

She tells me, "This spirituality, this meditation is much more powerful than anyone has ever imagined for it is very ancient. We are all here to lend our own energy to those who seek this method. What more is there to look for?

"This spirituality and meditation is what can really help humanity help themselves, but first they must become aware of it. That is why my book is so important. Only then can they realize how easy it is to save the planet and humanity, and how very little effort it will take.

"Therefore, we need courageous souls like you and many others that have no fear of speaking out and speaking the truth, Humanity is more than ready for this truth. It is now getting to the point where nothing else remains that can save your planet from certain catastrophe.

"Many have searched almost everywhere, and have not found a satisfactory solution. Of course they did not realize the solution was always within themselves, because that was too simple. That would be the last place anyone would look. It has always been within you.

"That has been your little gift. This is your soul that you received when you came into this physical body. It is your greatest gift. Few ever searched, or looked or appreciated it, but everything is in this little gift.

"Look at it as a little golden jewelry box wrapped with a golden ribbon. You can open it, and you will never tire of unpacking and packing, because it contains everything that you will ever need. All your needs is within this little golden jewelry box!"

Christina said, "In other words it is bottomless,"

She tells me, "You are funny, but you understand what I am trying to tell you."

Christina said, "I try to be a good listener and a good student."

She tells me, "You are special. I wish you had not taken so long to finally get to this point. But this is where your free will and your own choices have taken you up to this point. You have always been free. You needed time to learn and grow. Your way to the light came through your making those choices.

"It is what you call a spiritual growth as well as a physical. One cannot exist without the other. You had to harm your physical body before finally listening to your spiritual.

"But at last you finally listened to your spiritual body. Many never do. They never become aware that they could save themselves for it is never too late. Everything is so simple and easy. It is like being lost in a thick forest, trying to find shelter when it is all around you. Sometimes you are spiritually blind and cannot see."

She tells me. "My new book will help many. When they read my words and those of the other angels, they will know that this is the truth. All they have to do is follow their vibrations, and they will be guided to it on their soul level. For those that are searching, the soul level will rise above the physical and the physical will follow.

"This is why this book is so very important and that we all must work on it together, especially those of you who have promised. You must do it in peace, with your heart filled with love and harmony."

Christina said, "She is holding up this book and I see it. She is sitting on a cloud with a globe under her feet and a rose in her hands."

She tells me, "I am going to lend my energy to this book, And from its pages will come my contribution to everyone on earth—to all humanity. This book will contain my unconditional love and that of the angels. We are giving humanity a choice, perhaps a last choice.

"It will be their choice, and many will want to make the right one when they read this book. The world is waiting for this information. They have been waiting for its simplicity and understanding. It will enable them to begin applying this knowledge to their own lives. They will know that it will work for them. They have become weary and tired.

They cannot tolerate much more pain and suffering. In this they will find a solution to that pain and the agony that comes with it.

"I am looking at humanity as fragile and tired human beings, in desperate need of spiritual nourishment. What we now offer will put many of their lives back on the right path."

Christina said, "I see her rose unfolding again. I always feel like I have earned another little point in my spiritual life, I know I have grown a little during this session."

Mother Mary said, "Yes."

Christina replied, "I feel like this is my reward. Thank you so much Mother Mary. I am so happy to help and I know everyone else is happy to help for they also feel your love. That is the greatest gift I could ever receive from you.

As Mother Mary faded out of our view, Christina relaxed quietly in her chair, resting in the bliss from the long spiritual contact. A peaceful sleep will soon follow.

Tschen Li had given us a lot more to think about in his description of the catastrophes in store for our own beloved earth. Mother Mary had given additional information about the relationship between the physical body and spiritual. Only a few have allowed themselves to come into balance. It is a balance we must attain and maintain.

The Power of One Thought

Through the first half of this book, Mother Mary and the other angels have, in direct conversations with Christina, given us a large quantity of information. In their spoken thoughts, ideas and observations, they have given us a clear picture of our own earth as they see and understand it.

In these sessions, they have given Christina instructions on how she could help prevent, or at least alleviate, the earth's natural consequence from mankind's misuse of its resources. They even take it further in including the consequence of our pursuit of the physical and neglect of the spiritual, or the inner self sometimes called the soul.

Their thoughts on the subject speak for themselves. But in this chapter, they become more specific to the point that it can become somewhat alarming, which is their call to action. But always, they show us how we can avoid the consesequence of what we are doing.

In all of these solutions, _The Power of One Thought,_ stands above all others as one possible benefit.

Christina and I have just arrived at the entrance of the Temple of Knowledge.

Christina said, "And the doors are open. I am picking up these wonderful supportive vibrations from everyone."

They said, "So you have finally come. We have been waiting."

Christina said, "They so much want as many as possible to come, but not everyone can come here. To do so, one has to be able to lift his or her vibrations to this level, after attaining the ability to visualize and to make contact. Only then can they enter this realm."

The angel's said, "Many would like to come but they

can't quite make it. We know because we have been there and it was difficult for us until we were finally able to shed our physical bodies and come here in our spiritual. None of us were able to come in here until we did that.

"We are all here to learn now, but you both are so advanced and it is important that you come here as often as possible for you also need to learn.

"There is so much for you to do. Everything comes to order in the divine plan and this order is here now. You are directly connected with the divine plan, for everyone is connected and has it within themselves."

Christina said, "They are singing this lovely tune. It is just glorious! I am taking my seat in front. The vibrations are just wonderful, just penetrating. Now I hear almost like a choir in the background. It is an angelic choir. It is almost like a sacred kind of singing.

"I feel like these melodies are wrapping around us, and embracing us. It is a profound feeling, of great love, of great affection. That is so powerful, it brings tears to my eyes.

"I see Mataji coming. She calls me, my dear one, I am happy to see you."

She tells me, "The time has come to work together. There is not much time left to waste, and I am sure you are very much aware of it. We all have our part to do. This is the beginning.

"Unfortunately there are so very few that want to come and spend this time with us and want to help. There are not many and this is the big problem. But you both can make a great difference for you have to reach out and help everyone who wants to raise their vibrational level.

"It is so important for many will perish, and there is

actually no need for it to happen. But nobody wants to make the effort, and nothing gets done without making an effort, nothing! The only way your soul can fulfill its promise, and learn about humanity is by getting involved and doing it.

"That is why we are so pleased that you are both making this effort along with many others. But first those that are working with you must learn to raise their vibrational level much higher. It is like plugging into this outlet to receive electricity, only some cannot find this outlet no matter how hard they try. Others are not willing to search for the supply source. They want everything to come to them the easy way.

"Yet, everything is so simple. It only takes a little time and effort. Everyone can achieve the same level, but they must want to. We can only reach down to a certain level, the rest is up to you.

"Your soul is willing to help. Your soul wants to get up to the highest vibrational level. It has a yearning to get higher and higher, but it cannot do it alone. The physical body has to help. It is like the physical body is the plug that needs to make connection to the electrical outlet.

You have to be stronger in sharing this message with the others. They are starting to understand and want to know more. Their determination must become stronger. They must become dedicated and want to go all the way. You must show them the way. You must reach out more.

"This is all you can do, just show them. They have to go onto this path themselves. You are to teach them, send them love, give them support. You know you have done this many times before! The stronger you become in this, the more you get in touch with your own soul level. And as in each of these sessions, the more we can reveal to you."

"And you will write about these contacts in your book, Everyone that reads it will learn the same facts, and the same lessons that you receive. You have been a good teacher before, and you can do it again. Just do it!"

"And to your student, Gregorio, you can do the very same thing. I don't have to remind you! I know you are willing, but you are not willing enough to open up. You must make this effort, you can no longer keep it for yourself. This is your time to open up. You must help. You must learn to overcome these many painful obstacles.

Christina said, "She is telling me that he understands very well. It is so important now, for we are all in this together. We all promised before we left and if we do not keep our promises, we will come back on a much lower level, and this will be very painful!

"She is telling me how much love she has for us, how we have had this love long before we came into this body! And our love must become strong again. It must prevail. Only then can we overcome and be this strong being and again accomplish everything that we know, but there again it takes effort!

"I can feel <u>Mother Mary</u> coming in. She tells me welcome my child. How glad I am to see you. This is a very special day in my life. She is looking very seriously at me and I don't know why.

"She tells me I must become more firm in my teaching, in my sharing this message. We no longer have time to just explain, it is a matter of doing it. She is almost pleading with me."

She is saying, "Little one, it really is time. Your planet is crying out, and it almost cannot stand the pain anymore. It is becoming so weary and so fragile. Your planet has to be saved. And it can be saved, but you can no longer just explain. From now on, do not just explain, tell them what needs to be done."

And she tells me, "As for Gregorio, tell him he also promised. And you must also do your part, but it is not you alone. No! You must open and share with all the others. You cannot do it on your own. You must share. We are in this together.

"You must open up, you must grow, and let this love come in and embrace it. Only then can you heal! This pain you are feeling is the pain not only from yourself but also from the planet. Unless we can heal all, there cannot be any salvation. And in order to heal we must open up, we must embrace everything, whether it fits our needs or not.

"We have to become more tolerant. Sometimes unconditional love is not enough. There has to be an understanding on all levels. All levels. There has to be an opening and releasing on all levels!"

And she tells me, "When you need this help, when you need our support, just visualize my love. Visualize my understanding.

Visualize my embrace. I will always be there for you, and you will always have the courage to do whatever you have to do.

"You know fear must <u>never</u> enter any corner of your being. I have so much love to give, but very few ask for my love, for my help, for my understanding. I understand everything, and I want to help. I want to help all of you, but you have to open up. You have to reach higher to this vibrational level in order for me to embrace you!

"You know you can make this difference. Everyone who

comes here to this level can make a difference. We don't need many, but in order for every soul to grow and develop and expand it has to come to this level.

"Most souls are in a prison of a human body, and are in pain and agony. I am very much aware of that, but there is nothing I can do! Please children, help. Remember what you promised. And one day you will get your reward."

She tells me, "Do your part by telling them that it is time. It is also never too late for anyone who desires to come, but they have to want to, not because you asked them. They have to want to. They have to ask. No one else can do their work. Every soul has the responsibility.

"Every soul has to do their own growing along with the physical body. For the physical body also has to evolve and grow. All of you have made great progress and all of you have helped many, but you have to do more. And there is so much more to be done. This will be an endless learning experience!

"Endless, for it will not change when you come back to our level. It will be an endless evolution, an endless time of growing, an endless love."

Christina asked, "In other words, am I to understand that there will never be a period of no, never. This is endless! There is no beginning, there is no end, it is endless!"

"Mother is telling me that she could with one thought change our whole planet into a beautiful paradise, but then we would have all failed. No one would have learned anything, and no one would want to live in a form of slavery. Every one wants to be free.

" So she tells me if I can do this with one thought, all of you can now do more than you think with one thought. Everyone has the power within them, but they have to

activate this thought, after they learned how to accomplish
it. They earn the right to use it.

Christina asked, "So if we all would have the thought
form to heal our planet, it could actually happen.?"

She tells me, "Of course! The power of your mind is
endless because it is connected with the higher vibrational
levels. But since most thought forms are dark and negative,
earth has ended up with a severe problem. That difficulty
has brought on earth's present emergency.

So she is telling me, "Impress upon those you teach that
positive thought forms, even happy thought forms, kind
thought forms, loving thought forms are supporting and
expanding these vibrations. That will also help the planet to
become more balanced.

"This is nourishment for the planet. This adds to the
essence of what the planet needs. Like the tree of life, its
energy increases exponentially. Everything works together!
It is so simple and yet the majority won't accept it because it
is simple!"

Christina said, "She is telling me that this is what I must
stress, the simplicity of everything. That is what makes it
work. Not difficult. Quite different from the guru-type life
styles, or the other unbalanced teachings that abound out
there. Simplicity, purity, strength, and togetherness, just tie
it all together and do it!"

She tells me, "This is why my book will be so important!
It will spell out simplicity. It will spell out purity! It will also
spell out strength on all levels. All of you must get together
and in a very loving and caring way, you must fulfill this
wish I have, for you have also promised! You must fulfill
this wish, all of you.

"This will be like a golden key. This will be the key to

open the door! And many will find this key in this book! And I will lend my energy!"

Christina said, "Mother Mary, we will do all we can, I promise. I know I will.

She tells me, "For only then can you have your rewards, and one day it will become very clear to all of you. One day, for this was very much a part of you before you left, and when you return it will again become a part of you. Only then will it become a stronger part of you, for you will have risen to higher levels. You have become stronger."

"She shows me a bouquet of love. It is a bouquet, its not flowers its just love and this bouquet of love has all the colors of the rainbow. She is giving it to me and she tells me, when you are very sad, envision this bouquet of love and she will be in those colors, and just let it embrace me."

She said, "This is my little gift."

Christina said, "I will never be able to handle all of this."

"And she said, "Yes, you will, together you will, for this is the way it has to be. You have to become strong for you promised to help. Joshua needs your help, remember we are all in this together. You have much help now, and you know what you can use to penetrate all those that need your help and want your help.

"Do not waste your time on others, for they will never learn. They will never learn! She is smiling at us and telling us not to forget her message. It is very important!"

She slowly moves back to the right side of the stage. As she fades away, Christina and I sit pensively in our chairs. In deep meditation, we relax. Our minds scan the glorious scenes, the predictions and the love we have just shared with the angels. I know we both and others will do all we can to help.

The Angels Voice Concern

As our meditative visits to the Temple of Knowledge continue, additional angels come for short visits. Many of them add their own views about the damage mankind is doing to our planet.

The opinion of our first visitor today is no exception. His identity is exceptional since he is among the best known of all the angels who have something to say on the same subject. He opened his contact with Christina by telling her, and through her to everyone, his thoughts and opinions.

I repeat his words as she spoke them while in an intense moment of mental contact. I sit in solemn awe and wonder, my meditative contact lifting my inner awareness to levels never before considered possible. In those moments of bliss, I asked the angels to grant me the ability to allow you to share the special feelings of spiritual bliss that now hold me in their arms.

Christina is saying, "I see <u>Jesus</u> coming in."

He tells me, "It is time now, my little one, your planet is in much danger. You must try to reach out more. You must try to make them aware that if they do not change their life style, it will become very dark on their planet.

"This darkness will consume much. It will consume part of your planet along with humanity, and everything else that is alive. The cleansing has to take place.

Christina says, "I see this darkness like a huge spider, eating everything that is alive, that is of flesh. All is falling apart and this huge spider is eating everything that is within its reach and grasp.

"And that spider is the darkness, the negativity that will devour everything that is weak. Everything that is not strong enough to resist."

He tells me that, "No one will be aware of when the time comes. Those who do not heed our warnings will just be surprised when the natural consequence of their neglect takes place. Then it will be too late. Many of us continue to give warning, but only few take notice.

"Among them are the few that are connected with you at your high level. You must continue to make them aware, on all levels. You will be shown the way, but you will have to help others that want to, but could not find the way. We will continue to help, but you are aware that from this level we have our limitations."

And he tells me, "Of those who listen, very few want to make the effort. But time is moving on your planet. We live in a timeless state. We could say it will be later on, but for us a day could be as much as a thousand years to you."

Christina said, "I don't pick up that the angels know the time limit. They only wait for the Divine Plan. And when all is within the Divine Order, it will happen. What is coming to me is the beginning will be in the near future."

He tells me, "Knowing that is not important. But you, my little one, will be aware, and you will be there to help others. For more will come to you when the end time becomes more apparent."

Christina said, "But this is only my simple interpretation. I could be wrong. And I get this very heavy dark feeling that it's not going to be easy. It will be devastating. I get that there will be little left to support life on our planet. And all of their materialistic gains will not help them."

He tells me. "We have no use for that up here. We want for all of you to change your ways. To turn around and move toward the light. To seek out the perfect balance between the physical and spiritual. And there are only a few moving in that direction at this time.

"Everyone is in such a state of confusion that they have become insensitive. They are not even aware that there is a much better way of surviving, and a better way of living. It's like they are all in a dungeon and can see no way out. And they will all suffocate in there.

"Witness the air around you, what will they do when it will no longer sustain life?"

Christina said, "I see myself floating around the outside of this dungeon. and there is no way I can get in. I hear them scream and yell in agony, and I can't get in. And those that give me the vision tell me that at that time there will be nothing that I can do to help. They had their chance, and they made their own choices. And now they have to live or perish with those choices"

He says, "When this is all over with, there will be a much lighter and life-sustaining atmosphere. Everything will be much more balanced, and everyone still living at that time will be much more spiritual, loving and caring.

"Of course, you will not have those advanced toys you now have become accustomed to. You need to go back to the primitive way of existence."

Christina said, "That's all right. We will be fine. This is what we will have to do to begin again. And I see that only a few of us will be up here, gathered together to help in any way we can. Even then, we can make a difference. We can help. We will be guided and protected by the angels. And the mountains will be our refuge."

And he is looking up at me and telling me, "Remember this lecture. Listen to it over and over again. You must be aware and you must prepare. Remember that everything in creation has to live in harmony with God's unconditional love. Teach everyone to seek it and make it their own."

He tells me, "I will always watch over you."

Christina said, "He is now slowly moving back into the shadows. Only one thing can fill the void left by his departure, I feel Mother Mary coming in.

"She is not sitting, but standing this time. Her usual happy smile is missing. She appears very sad.

"She tells me, "Welcome, my child. I am pleased that you are here. I am happy that you have made this cause your own, and you are doing what you want to do, not because it's what we want you to. I wished there were more like you,"

Christina said, "There will be more, I am sure."

She tells me. "Yes, I know, but time is of the essence, we don't have very much of it left."

Christina said, "You are always telling me that Mother, but what does it really mean. How is time of essence. How does time have so much importance in everything we do?"

She tells me, "The negativity and the problems that you have on your planet are gaining in strength and this means that more and more of you need to be sending light and energy and healing.

"You cannot let the forces of darkness get much stronger. You cannot let them become strong enough to devour you too. We have to gain in number and determination, as well and become strong."

And she tells me "There are many, many dark places and they are getting darker as well as stronger. And it is so important that we do everything that we can to save your planet from destruction. You must get more involved. You must send more healing and energy."

And she tells me, "Even some of your so-called religious leaders are becoming weaker. They are not raising the vibrational level of the souls they teach. They are also being enticed by material desires. They are losing the clear picture of what they should be teaching, and spending too much time talking about what they call evil forces. The fear they are generating creates more darkness in an area where there is too much already.

"It's like they are losing their strength so therefore all of the teachings that they are doing is of a very low and poor quality which doesn't help any because they are pulling all these souls down with them just for the power and gain."

Christina said, "So, what's left mother, what's left?"

And she tells me, "Very little. All these souls that are on the higher vibrational levels are the ones that will be on safe grounds because they are the ones that will continue once the destruction has taken place. They will remain strong and they will help others who want to get back onto this level. It is going to be a, I want to say, loosing battle."

But she tells me, "It cannot be lost, it has to be saved. There is so much to live for on this planet. This planet cannot be destroyed. There are too many souls out there that want to continue making this a better place to live. You have to help find them, and get them more involved. We will help you all that we can."

Christina said, "I see what you plan for us to do. We will have to join together, we have to talk, show our concerns. This is how we can make ourselves stronger, and rise above personal desires to see the complete picture of what we are faced with. We have to get everyone involved that we are in contact with. Than can we can become this one very strong group in our little corner of the world,"

She tells me, "That alone will make such a great difference. Many are already perishing on your planet, and few are even aware of it. She calls it the silent perishing, the tragedy no one even knows about. Her only pleasure is in the fact that their souls are finally free and can come back home. There they can heal and eventually come back to earth again and inhabit another body for hopefully a better and more uplifting life than they had before, if that is their choice."

But she tells me, "Many souls still on earth are hurting. They are crying out for help, but they also know that they are helpless, there is nothing anyone can do until they are free, out of this prison of a body that is even indifferent to its existence."

Then she tells me, "When it occurs, it will happen quite unexpectedly. Everyone will be totally surprised. Its like they would say, 'we didn't expect it to come this quickly. We thought that if it did really happen, it would take place much later than this, or not in our time.'

"But that is due to your wrong teachings, and wrong predictions. The true knowledge of what will come cannot even exist in the sullied atmosphere presently existing on planet earth. When it comes, it will happen unexpectedly. All of the predictions about the end-time that fill the information circuit are going to be proven wrong."

Christina said, "Are you aware of the time?"

Mother Mary said, "It is not important that you know the exact time. Be assured that it will happen, and when it comes, the time will be when we least expect it.

"Remember the parable about the shepherd's concern for one lost sheep. For nearly two thousand years, along with other angels, I have shared the same concern over one lost planet. It's a long time for a mother to watch and pray over a planet full of her wayward children. If only they could realize what they have done and have not done, and what they have promised.

"Some are aware that the time is becoming short, yet they keep procrastinating and saying. 'Well, it will be a while or it will happen next year, or next month or not in my lifetime.'

"Well, it is here now. "It is much more severe than we can even imagine, much more severe. But do not even think of fear, do not even think of destruction, just be aware of how bad our situation is and do all you can to stay on this high vibrational levels. There you can reach down and bring up as many as you can find that have the desire to want to come up to this level.

"It will take very, very strong souls, because they have become so weak. Their genes have been poisoned so much that they can almost not detect when they are weak and when they are strong. That is your problem.

"This is why a new race has to emerge from the ashes of the present, because if it doesn't this will be the end of everything. And in the Divine Plan, it is not yet time for that.

"In the future, there will be a merging of the people of many other planets with those of your planet and this is where your greatest help will come from. But in order to receive this help you must develop the ability to tune into their high frequency. And that can only be done by those of you who have reached this higher level of vibrations."

"She is telling me that this is the only way she sees to help our planet. There are many planets that have succeeded where earth has failed. Help will finally come from another strong, pure, highly evolved race. They are the ones that will help you, and they will only make contact with the higher vibrational souls."

She tells me. "And you will be one of them. And don't be surprised if you will have contact soon because it has to happen. And there again it will happen when you least expect it. Just know and be aware of it. Your soul will recognize it and you will know what you have to do. Soon you will know."

She tells me, "Now you know the truth. Everyone knows that your whole planet is out of balance. This is why you have the extremely severe weather in a cycle that is not normal. It cannot come back into balance until after the cleansing.

"It is too much on one side, and not enough on the other. And then, there is all this darkness around it and until this planet is back in balance, it will continue on this cycle. There again, because of these serious weather conditions, many will also perish.

"This is also another part of the cleansing program. The other cleansing program will be because of the dark forces putting all this rage and hate and hostility into some of the bodies that are on a very low level, and the bottom line is they will disintegrate. And this is another problem we are having on your planet; the terrible hate, the greed and this will also be a part of the cleansing.

"Their physical bodies have been taken over by these forces, so completely they cannot breathe freely any more. And once the physical body reacts all on its own, without the spirit to guide it, then it becomes the lowest of the low. And that spells nothing but certain destruction. Far below animal level, one finds nothing but darkness and ultimate destruction."

Christina said, "That is horrible but I know what you are talking about Mother, I see it every day all around me. I know it happens. It does exist. It isn't something new that you are just telling me. I have known for a long time."

"But," she tells me, "it is out there in such greater measure, we can't even imagine. This is why I am urging all of you to please reach out, become strong, stay together. Form a good healthy, strong, spiritual group. It doesn't matter how little or how big, but stay together and do it together. That is what is important.

"It cannot be done by just one person, because there are many out there that need the support of the others. We have to support each other in order to remain on the level that we are on, because it is so easy to fall off of the path, and many of them struggle so hard, but there is so much enticement out there that unless you are very, very strong and sure of yourself, and make this commitment, you don't even know that you are falling off."

"And," she tells me, "you had this experience with a very good friend of yours, a lovely soul and I am happy with what you did for her. Now it is up to her to remain strong. She has much negative force around her and she must detect which is the good, and which is the bad level. Then she needs to choose sides, only then can she grow above it and help her loved ones. If she does not know, it will be her destruction too.

"This is why, souls like hers need your support, your help, your love and constant reaching out for, but you cannot do it for the soul. With our help, the soul has to do it itself, but you can be there and help, and support."

Christina said, "It all makes so much sense because I

have gone through it, I have lived through it. I have done it, but she is emphasizing this whole mission again. It makes my heart so heavy."

And she tells me, "Yes, I know. But it is not your fault, it is not your individual problem. Everyone has to take responsibility for themselves, just like you take responsibility for yourself. But the unconditional love has to be there for everyone else who is seeking this help, and the faith has to be there to enable you to do it.

"It doesn't matter what condition, what situation, you can do it. With your faith and unconditional love, you can literally move mountains."

Christina said, "She is telling me that it is important that I hear this many more times, because we need this constant reminder. If we don't have it, but maybe just once a week, or once a month, we forget the seriousness of our situation. It needs to be brought up over and over again so that we really will do something about it, and that we are constantly aware of it.

"Its like the rain that falls onto the earth, we don't have to look at it, but we are constantly aware of the rain when it is there. Its this little gentle nudge, and we know that if we want to remain dry, we have to prepare and cover up properly."

She tells me, "And this is how it is with this situation. You have to constantly be aware of it, and prepare and protect yourselves. To make this commitment is so very, very important.

"Unless you make this commitment you are not going to accomplish anything. The commitment is what lets you do everything that you need to do on a constant and even level. Only then can we become successful.

Christina said, "Oh, Mother Mary!

"Yes," she tells me, "it is sad, it is very sad, but we all must do our part. And in so doing, we will earn our rewards, our credits. What you are doing here for your planet, will be recognized when you come back home.

"This is where your actual soul growth begins, through these good deeds that you are doing for your planet. This is how your soul can evolve to higher levels, and this will be your reward.

"This is where the terms old soul and new soul comes in. The old soul has learned many lessons. It was able to grow to greater heights, and those deeds or credits that you are earning there also support the growth of your soul level. And this is where your soul will develop into ever higher and higher levels. In time, your soul will achieve what is called Mastership."

Christina said, "She is smiling at me, and she tells me I know what you are thinking."

"Why not?" Christina asked. "Is it so far ahead of where I am now? And after all this time, why is Ralph not also?"

And she tells me, "Of course, it will come in time. As for Ralph, he earned it long ago. He thinks that in working from this level, he will empathize much better with those around him."

Christina asked, "So all the treasures that we have on our planet mean absolute zero, nothing, and the majority of humanity on our planet are building only their planetary credits."

And she said, "Of course. While you are in that body, you must take care of it. You should keep it just as pure, and as clean, and as healthy as your soul. In order to do that, your physical body has to be nourished.

"You need to have shelter, a balanced environment. In order to do this, you need to do all the other things that are required. You must always stay in the realm of purity, of balance, of happiness.

"You must never forget why you are here, or your purpose in life. You must keep the temple of your soul in a healthy and pure condition. And you must never be enticed in any way to deviate away from this balanced, harmonious level.

"And this will be a constant struggle. Because almost daily, the struggle you are having, you are constantly being deceived by almost everyone. If you maintain your high level of consciousness, your intuition will enable you to immediately detect anything not in your best interest.

"It is for your best interest to raise your soul level, your physical level to the highest possible level. Sometimes the little creatures of deception are very insidious' making them almost impossible to detect unless you remain constantly alert.

"They are very insidious like a small cancer that begins to attach itself to a part of your body. You push the small annoyance aside. You know something is wrong, but it is only a minor inconvenience. But if you neglect early treatment, soon it will become so large it cannot be healed. Without early treatment, it could become untreatable. And you know what that means."

Christina said, "Oh, that is a horrible analogy."

She tells me. "That cancer must never ever enter your body. And it will not if you remain strong and faithful. And that should be everybody's goal."

She tells me, "Now, my little one, I must tell you a

happy story. Soon, you will be filled with a great deal of happiness. It will lead you to higher and higher levels of vibration. You will be recognized as a very highly evolved soul. And I, for one, am happy that I was able to help and save one of my children!"

Christina said, "So am I,"

She continued, "I am also very happy and your rewards will be many. Just stay strong my child, keep your commitment, keep your faith and do what comes naturally. Do what you feel you have to do, and let nothing stop you.

"This is your soul that you have to nurture. This is your quest and it will eventually lead you to where you need to go. Stay strong and I will always be there for you!"

Christina said, "Thank you, Mother Mary. I love you too. She is leaving now."

Christina and I remained quietly seated in our chairs. We were filled with awe over what they had just revealed. Still in deep meditation, we watched Mother Mary move slowly off to the right and fade away, taking our love and emotions with her.

We allowed memories of what they told us to fill our minds with the awful significance of the revelations they left with us. Yet, from within all of the information they had just given us, there always came the promise *if.* What they predict for the future is immanent, if we can't get enough people of help us do what all of them promised before they entered into this lifetime.

From what I see in the problems of earth and its environment, we still have enough time to alter the destructive forces that threaten our planet. We will have to act fast, and get this message into the hands of those who are anxious to help us make that change before it becomes too late.

And in this meditation, you will find the knowledge and the ability to make it happen.

Just remember, when you read these messages. If you feel the need to add your thoughts and actions to those who are already working with the angels, this book will show you the way.

Every soul existing in the eternal presence of God, and filled with that unconditional love, is contributing a positive energy into the force-field of the Light Workers who labor for the good of us all.

More Predicted Changes

The minds of the angels that speak to us so often now, are in total contact with the infinite mind that is Creation. That spiritual contact places them in harmonious contact with all knowledge that was, is, and the Divine Plan of what will be.

Theirs is not a call to alarm. It is rather an indication of what could happen if enough of us do not awaken to the problem and add our voices and our efforts to work toward finding a solution.

They do not criticize. They also offer us some workable solutions. They point out methods we could use to make our lives more meaningful, and helpful to those around us with whom we share earth's living space.

The first five pages of this lesson finds Christina visiting a mammoth crystal cave as we arrived at that special planet. There we find our old friend, Aliathor. The liaison between the crystal world and that of humanity.

In his presentation of the many wonders of this special location, we are privileged to experience a sense of wisdom and feel the healing power of the enormous quantity and quality of the crystals. All of that and more, makes a visit to this place of wonder a must for every person we bring with us to this location.

When combined with the special energy and healing methods we find in this location, it presents one out of the many methods the angels offer as possible solutions to earth's problems.

During the remainder of this session, the angels continue to give Christina more instructions, along with additional information that should be of interest to us all.

Christina said, "As I enter into the crystal world, I am standing beside Aliathor. He is explaining to me the importance of the energy of these crystals. We are fortunate the angels guided us here—the only way for us to finally merge our consciousness with the special awareness that the angels call The All—the ultimate vibration.

"The extraordinary power within these crystals can help you with their special energy and healing. It is of such capacity, we cannot even begin to comprehend its extent.

"The crystal itself produces the male energy that all of us need to periodically renew, refine, and reattune ourselves to the infinite energies of the universe.

"The emerald produces the female energy. It is a much gentler and softer energy that is equally as important to everyone as is the crystal energy.

"And ahead of me is a massive open cone made of amethyst. It is taller than me, and at this level of awareness I can walk into it and merge with it in perfect comfort. It surrounds and embraces my entire being.

"These Amethyst crystals vibrate at the frequency of one's spiritual being. In so doing, it furnishes and replenishes our own spiritual energy, and continues to aid in our spiritual development.

"It emanates the highest color in the visible spectrum. It represents the highest level of that part of the energy, and it is used for spiritual growth and development. As I am standing here, I can feel the energy penetrating into my being. It is like electricity going through me. This energy is so important to everyone.

"As I continue to stand in here, I can feel the energy filling my chakras. They are being loaded with an energy that is only spiritual, for my own development. It is so overwhelming, I can only stay in here a little while, and I enjoy every minute of it. Finally, I am walking back out.

"Now I am standing in front of Aliathor. He tells me how important these crystals are. I am picking up from him that this energy is the only nourishment we need for the spiritual existence of our mind and body.

"This is all they need. They require nothing else but this energy. This is how they mentally perform everything that needs to be done. This is how closely we need to work with all of them. This is the driving force for the spiritual body.

"It is not enough to have a gem in front of you, or to hold it or wear it. It is important to mentally merge with these gems, for this is how you pick up the vibrations and the energy for the spiritual body. That is what is so very important, and very few even know. I don't think that anybody has ever written anything on that subject. It is not even known. This knowledge is only available in contact with this world and at this level of consciousness."

He tells me, "First you have to lift your vibrations to get to this level of the crystal cave. Only then will you begin to receive the knowledge."

Christina said, "And he is the master and keeper of all of these crystals. For they are so ancient, I cannot even pick up a time. And I have a feeling that these crystals were instrumental in the creation of our planet, and possibly to create many other planets. This is how powerful they are.

"And I feel that there's much more to it, more than I can even comprehend."

And he is smiling at me, like, "You are picking up very well, my child."

Christina said, "He doesn't say anything. He just smiles at me, but I know that kind of a look. In other words, I have the feeling that I have to pick this information up for myself through these vibrations. And this is how I will develop.

"In other words this is not just the answer to a problem that is handed to me. I have to pick it up for myself. This is part of my learning experience.

"This is why it is so important to come here, and to bring the right kind of people here. Then they can first of all lift their vibrations to these extremely high levels, and when they reach high enough, they can tune in to the crystal knowledge. I guess I have made enough progress in order to pick that up for myself."

I am being told, "No, as you come here, you are remembering more and more, from a time in the past when you were very familiar with this subject. This used to be your favorite place. And you know the reason why, don't you?"

And I am also picking up. "That anyone who is very low in energy could come here and merge with these crystals. They can be healed if they but let this energy penetrate their being.

"It's not only a matter of doing, it's a matter of just believing and then doing. This energy has an awareness of its own. It is very intelligent. It knows exactly where it needs to be. It is much more intelligent than many of our human brains can ever be. There is no comparison between them. If they are intelligent enough to create new planets, then we are but a speck of dust!

Now Aliathor is looking at me and saying, "I am happy that you are on a high enough level to pick up this knowledge, for it is not easy. First of all you have to get used to the subtle energy. Then as you receive the energy, you look beyond the energy and that is where the knowledge is. Very few ever get beyond this energy. It is difficult just to even deal with the energy, let alone to get beyond it."

He is now embracing me and telling me, "How proud I am of where you are, how happy I am, but this is just the beginning of attaining the level of where you once were before you left."

Christina said, "I don't even have to say one word. With their energy and their mind, they know all there is.

"Slowly, I am floating back out toward the open level. and into this bright sunshine. Oh, how I love the energy that comes out of this sun. It is beautiful to see and feel. Why don't I feel the same about the sun on our planet. Our sun feels warm and hot and you cannot remain in its rays for long periods of time. But here, you can remain in this sunlight for hours, and it never gets too hot.

"These sun rays bathe you in their healing energy and in a perfect state of enjoyment at the same time. And I feel that this healing is for both the physical and the spiritual body. It is all very important to our physical body. But here, I am getting that this sun, like everything on this planet, has an intelligence that it uses to sustain and heal everything.

"I am getting that when we become adept in using the meditation that brings us here, we should spend as much of our spare time as possible in this area. Frequent vacations with the masters and angels in this area of creation will heal our bodies, our souls, and take our minds into unimaginable levels of consciousness. It is an overall improvement that we need desperately.

"I am looking at the lake in front of me, and at the mountains. And above the mountains I can see hundreds of the spiritual beings of this planet, floating above and around it. They seem very happy. As much as I try, I can ascertain no reason for their congregating in that area. I guess that for me, it is not important that I know the reason at this time.

"On my right, I see many homes made of crystal. About a hundred or so. They are all empty. I get the feeling that anyone that comes here can choose any home for their own.

As I approach the temple, I can hear Hildegard von Bingen, my friend from long ago, singing. She is singing Ave Maria again. She has such a beautiful voice. She is telling me through her vibrations, "Soon you will know why it is so important to listen to my vibrations. Your help will be needed. On your earth, someone will become very ill. I will be there to help you to choose the proper herbs for healing.

"All you have to do is make contact with me, then you will know exactly what to do. You have worked with me before when you were my little helper, and I have taught you much. And with my energy and my vibrations, you will remember again."

Christina continues, "We are moving through the open door of the temple and there are quite a few (angels) today. They are very happy to see me. They are always asking me, "Why have you not brought more?"

Christina said. "It is very difficult. There are very few that I know that can come to this high level. It's like many of them come so far and then they stop. It's like, they cannot come higher, or perhaps don't want to. Perhaps they don't have the energy. Maybe it's a combination of all.

"But to have no fear, and be totally free, and just let it happen, there are only a few that can come to this level with me, or can even reach this level. And through this level, and the energy received from these vibrations, it is so easy to let yourself go, and to float as high as you need to."

Christina continues, "I am floating easily down to the front row. I can feel the presence of my own two masters behind me. They are always there, but they blend in with the other light beings. I know exactly who they are, and where they are, for they have a different vibration. A much more subtle vibration, a stronger vibration than these other beings.

"Here they are all equal. Even though other beings still have to learn much, and my masters have exceeded them a long way, they are all the same, they are all equal here, like I am at this moment. We all have equal feelings of being, of love and togetherness.

"The place is very brightly lit today. I see <u>Tschen Li</u> coming over and giving me a big smile"

He is beaming his love at me and telling me, "Soon my little one, you will experience new heights, new vibrations. And it is your will to learn more, to reach higher levels, for the energy within you continues to become stronger. And the only way for that energy to grow is for you to continue reaching up for higher levels.

"You will also need those higher levels because of what is ahead of you. You have made very fast progress, but you always have. This is why we have chosen you along with others. You do follow through with your promise once you set your soul free.

"And this is what it takes to reach the highest level. It also requires commitment and dedication, and you have that. And with your knowledge, your energy, and your deep and simple dedication, you will bring many more to this level.

"For you will be our teacher on your planet. Of course, you have free will. You will also remember what you have promised."

Christina said, "I know, and I will always do your work on all levels I am worthy of. And I have a feeling that a strong illness, a devastating illness is already on our planet. It is a very infectious illness. And I am seeing all of these dominos in mid air, just falling down as one touches the other one.

"This is how rapidly this infection will hit. But if you are in total balance and harmony, and your spiritual body is in perfect order, it cannot penetrate. No matter how strong this illness or infection is, it can never penetrate a very balanced and harmonious body that has a strong auric field. For that is the protection for this vulnerable, heavy piece of flesh and bone that is your body.

"I almost have a distaste for this body because it can be so destructive to the soul. It can be so greedy and power hungry, I am almost to the point I am ready to give it up and return to the spiritual."

Tschen Li said, "Oh, my child, but it is very important, for your spiritual body alone cannot exist at this low level. Until you return back here where we are now, you must put up with it for a while longer. Those who have a strong spiritual body will not be affected at all.

"This is all the more reason for following the path of this meditation as you have done. Many who have not done so will not be so fortunate."

Christina said, "I see this very heavy smoke in the air, so you cannot see the sky or the sun. Everything is filled with this heavy gray smoke, and it's very hard to breathe.

"This, of course, is a vision they are sending me. I don't know whether it is a volcanic eruption, or if it is lack of oxygen from all of the poison that is around, that the sun cannot penetrate. And all of this is slowly choking us to death. It is choking the life out of our physical body.

"The body needs the pure air and oxygen. When this nourishment is no longer there, they are showing me everything just falling away, then there is nothing left but the spiritual body. The spiritual body ascends, and the physical body falls down into the dust.

"These are the two major catastrophes that I am being shown. And they are showing me that these occurrences are not too far away. And when it comes to pass, I see that everyone will be in a state of panic.

"But for most of them, it will be too late. They have done nothing to put their spiritual body in a position to help. And I am being shown them racing around in a panic, offering their hoards of silver, gold, and paper money to anyone who can save them, but no one can help."

He is telling me, "You cannot buy the strength and the power of spirituality with any of your materialistic wealth. You may think money can buy everything, but spirituality cannot be bought. It has to be earned by those who have found the road back, and faithfully follow that path to the highest level they could attain.

"At that high level you have anything and everything that you want. You will find that none of the negative vibrations found on earth can exist here."

Christina said, "And I am also being told that many will be coming to me for help, and that we have to be very selective. For some only come for their own selfish, materialistic gains. We only have time to help those who wish to attain the highest levels of spiritual contact, and come to us for the knowledge of how to get there. We can easily tell who they are by the sincerity of their vibrations and the radiant love surrounding them."

He tells me, "These fortunate people will always have one of the spiritual guides around to protect and support them. You will also know how to protect yourself so you will not be depleted by those around you. They are anxious to draw the strength out of you in a desperate effort to find something to save them from the hopeless situation they find themselves."

I asked Tschen Li, "Will it ever get any better?"

He sadly replied, "Not right away, my child. For that is only the beginning of earth's cleansing of all of the toxins and negativity. And it begins with mankind. After mankind has been sorted out, so to speak, and more and more of the negative ones have gone, the planet will begin to regenerate from its poison and negativity.

"At that point, the planet will not be as strong, and it can only slowly regenerate and recuperate. From our thinking, our working with the planet, it will not be as strong at that time. But with more and more of your positive thoughts and the good within mankind that is left on your planet, the more you will feed your planet on all levels with your thoughts, your doing, and with your actions. You will find that everything is connected. As above, so below."

Christina said, "Oh, Tschen Li, that is so sad."

And he tells me, "There should never have been any need for that. If only all would have remembered a little about where they came from and why they are here, and where they are returning to. For most fear that all there is to this planet is the materialistic way as the most powerful way, and there is nothing else beyond that but death."

Christina continues, "In other words, everything can be put in one little square, and they cannot see beyond this little square. For all is narrow and tunnel vision, and nothing exists beyond that square."

And he is telling me, "Now, you see, my little one, why it is so important to be there and help. You will be our connection for we cannot reach the others. I feel that I am in mid air between you and them."

Christina said, "I guess that's one way of seeing it and explaining it."

And he tells me, "This is very good. At least, you see, you feel, and you pick it up. I don't have to tell you that. But I expect nothing less from you."

And he is just beaming his eyes at me and saying, "Because of who you are, because of your knowledge, because of what I know about you, I knew we could count on you for your help. Of course, you always have free will. You have had it from the beginning, all of the way up to the time when you met my brother, Ralph..

"But you both have fulfilled your promise, and for that we are very grateful."

Christina continues, "Now I am seeing <u>Joshua</u> coming in, with his big, red and golden cape. I can see his sword glowing through the cape. And he tells me that much help has been given to him, for many are symbolically using the sword now."

He also tells me, "We have given our promise that even though we are not always there, we want everyone to use this sword for their own protection and that of your planet. It is only a symbol in the spirit world, but it is powerful enough to help everything on earth.

Christina says, "And I get this feeling of accomplishment. He feels that he is making headway now. And they are very grateful. He tells me that the darkness fills a large part of the planet. It is so devastating that the planet is actually rotting away because of all of this darkness and negativity.

"I see part of it falling off into this big black hole. So the planet must regroup, regenerate. It's like a cancer that had to fall off. And he is also sad in telling me that this could all have been prevented if only mankind had retained its connection with spirituality, with the other side. What we are doing now is not the reason we were brought onto this world.

"But we were given choices, and so many have made the wrong ones. They have chosen a path, and I see this path. It leads exactly toward the mountain. And when you reach it, you cannot go any further because you cannot walk through it. So the path is very short, and when you reach the mountain you come to a dead end. You are doomed, and that's all there is.

"They did not see the path that goes upward, and leads to eternity. Apparently they did not want to see it And now, Joshua is disappearing,"

Christina said, "And now I hear the wonderful music that's <u>Mother Mary</u> coming in. The energy I am receiving feels so good, a relief from the devastating messages I just received.

"She is now sitting in front of me with a blue veil wrapped around her body. She holds a beautiful rose, and of course, I am holding my own."

And she smiles at me and tells me. "All is not lost. As long as we have unconditional love for each other, as long as we want to help, you will always find us waiting when you return."

Christina said, "And I am picking up that we will make a

great difference in the lives of those that are coming to us. We will be able to help them. And even in the smallest way, it will be a help. And they will eventually find their own path, the right path.

"And all of this has been known from the beginning. Even then, they could not intervene."

She reminded me, "You were all given free will. You were all given choices. That was your test, your lesson to learn. Many have failed. If and when they return to earth, they must begin again in the most primitive way. They must work themselves back up to higher levels again.

"But those who have been on the path, and have been faithful and strong, will continue at the same level when they return. From there they can raise their vibrations to a much higher level where they will reap their rewards."

She smiles again as she tells me, "My heart is very sad. I am opening my heart. I am giving my love, but almost no one notices me. No one knows the feelings I have for every soul on earth. In fact, almost no one knows how easily I am to reach. My heart is very sad.

"There are many who are supposed to represent me, but if a highly advanced person like you would sense their shallow vibrations, you know that it cannot be me they claim to speak about. And this is the darkness that is poisoning mankind with its false teachings, and with their false prophesies. And it makes me very sad."

Christina said, "You know mother, because of many low level beings and their false prophesies, they cannot see above it or raise their levels above it. They cannot recognize or raise themselves above it to recognize the wrong prophecies and the darkness lurking behind them.

"And I am now seeing mother sitting way up there, and

some other beings way down but above the black hole. That is where they are, and that's the kind of erroneous material they believe in.

"She is very proud of my understanding, and that's why she is telling me that <u>My Book</u> is the only one that will save mankind. This is why it is so important to let it reach the many that are looking and wanting. This is her last offer to help, and time is not on our side. This book has to be out early next year. Within another year we will have less of a chance to prepare.

"She is pleading with me to please send out her message. The messages you received from me and the other angels that helped us write it, is clear and concise. Do not let anything else interfere. This is my unconditional love to all.

"She is so sad. She just hopes that we can see her sadness, and ask every one who cares to help us get her last message to mankind out to the world.

"And I have the feeling, Mother, that you already know the outcome.

"From the short distance separating us, I see a smile and feel her love, and the glistening ray of light from above reveals a glitter in the moisture in her eyes. As she slowly fades away, the final look of sadness on her beautiful face plunges my spirits into a state of loneliness that matches the nothingness left by her absence. She has now gone. I wonder if she will ever return."

Although Christina had developed the capability of coming to this level of awareness on her own, I had led her to the level of angelic contact. The angels, who now knew our every move, became aware of our actions when we began the meditation that would take us to that high level of celestial contact.

I saw every scene and heard every word of this special, extra long session. Mother Mary's good-bye left me in a state of sadness, and I made no effort to conceal my tears.

Christina wept softly, as if she had lost a very dear friend. I knew this was not our final meeting, although her sad departure might have indicated otherwise.

The angels, with their all inclusive knowledge of the cosmos, have to work under the laws of the Divine Plan and the Natural Laws of the Universe. They also have unlimited abilities. While dealing with humanity, they restrict the use of these abilities. To not abide by Universal Law, and allow mankind full use of his free will, would be unthinkable.

We who work with the angels, consciously strive to attain that same attitude. Our upward path is an expanding journey to the light, one filled with ever-expanding rewards that fill us with its bliss. When, like Christina, we make that final commitment, we are well on the way to attaining those angelic abilities.

Those who eventually attain to that level are called Masters—complete masters of themselves. For them, the gilt of earth's treasures has lost its luster. For nothing on earth could ever remotely compare to a life filled with the Eternal Presence of God.

In my formal training for this work, I had the good fortune to actually study under some of these masters during the remainder of their work on our planet. It always amazed me how they replaced authority with genuine love and interest in the well being of others, and how they recognized the genuine needs of others and helped quietly from a distance. Often those they helped were never made aware of their benefactor. That is unconditional love.

Like the angels, they had attained the ability to manifest

their physical needs with a single thought. I learned a valuable lesson when I observed them manifest no more than they actually needed, the only variation of that would be the presence of someone or a hungry bird or animal nearby.

When they make the final ascension over the Bridge to Eternity, they will live throughout Eternity in the Angelic Realm with the angels. That will be the final bliss.

They have promised that we who persevere can reach that same level of mastership. Every benefit we attain on our way up the path of spiritual evolvement is a powerful reward for attaining that level.

Knowledge that the final attainment of this study will be the prize of total mastership, should inspire everyone who begins this meditation to make that his or her final goal. It is a reward found only in personal contact with the angels. It has no equal in any other location except Creation.

The Present Situation

Two of our most powerful Angels, Mataji and Mother Mary, detail the immediate problems facing us, and how they interpreted our reaction to the information. Christina translated their thoughts as she received them from the angels, and interacted with them throughout the meditation. The entire session is presented here in first person mode. You can listen to the conversations and feel the sadness of the angels as they give us their messages.

Please remember that there are solutions that have been and will be given as we continue. We have the complete choice. It is up to us what we do about it.

We have completed the ascension, and arrived safely at the Temple of Knowledge. Relaxing comfortably in our favorite seats, the angels will soon appear.

Christina said, "I see a being of light coming out of the left side of the stage and it is Mataji. She wears a long golden gown that is more like a robe. She looks at me kind of sadly."

She tells me, "So far you are the only one that comes here with regularity and keeps their promise. You know that three others are coming also, but they have a long way to go. No one else has even tried.

"We want everyone to feel free to come, and there should be no fear ever of coming here. In the eternal presence of the Creator, the only sensation should be one of joy, and spiritual love. We want to help. Everyone on earth needs our help. It seems strange that only few have really made a serious effort. Which is really very sad.

"It seems most are not aware of how serious the situation on your planet is. But everyone has free choice and so far only a few have made the right one.

"I watched you teaching over this weekend and it pleased me to see how you brought your message across on the subject of healing the planet. This, of course, will help us greatly. Those who heard you will do their part, but only if you remain consistent. The rest will fall back into their former lifestyle.

"Those on our level that are concerned know that you have tried, and you have shared the messages we have given you. As you continue to teach, there will be many more. We know that we can count on you to do your part.

"I know you will do what you promised. In time, as you grow onto higher vibrational levels, your teaching will also move into those levels. It will not go unnoticed, either on our level or on the earthly plane. You will find this to be the beginning of a new life for you. Many have already noticed the great change in you. But then again you are special."

Christina said, Thank you Mataji."

Mataji said. "There is only one way to be grateful, and that you have done on your own. You have made the right choice and you have taken the right path, You could have chosen the other way, but of course you have a good teacher. And Ralph is that wonderful teacher.

"So you see, everything works with the Divine Plan. If you want the Divine Plan to work as planned, you must let it work with you and for you.

"Ralph has been with this plan for a long time and always tried to choose the right path. You must learn to do the same thing, for this will guide and protect you. Only then can we be with you. Only then can you achieve the level your soul so much wants to be on. For it also has the desire to grow."

Christina said, "What a wonderful message Mataji." She tells me, "I want so much to share this with many, many others. This is very sad for me for we all want to help humanity. We have so much love for everyone, but the many show very little desire for this love. Only the few seem to care."

Christina said, "In other words you are telling me that the human side, the materialistic side of humanity, is more prevalent, is more overpowering than the spiritual."

She tells me, "For them, yes. This is why humanity has fallen so low. No one wants to work for it, and nothing comes easy. Everything has to be earned. But we are happy we have reached you and many others, and they all have voluntarily come back to join us, if only but for a brief moment, while we connect on the spiritual realm.

"There is so much to learn, little one, so much to know, so much to hear. We can only teach you one part at a time. Then you can understand and work with it. As you develop and grow into higher vibrational levels, you will be able to understand more and more. It will no longer be over your head, as you call it.

"You know I always send you my love, my energy, my harmony, and my purity, especially when we merge. This is also part of your continued growth. The time will be here much sooner than you think. You will need to be strong, but you will never have to face it alone. One of us will always be there with you!

Christina said, "Thank you, Mataji. She answers with a loving smile on her face as she slowly moves to the back of the stage and disappears.

"Now, as she leaves us, I see the figure of <u>Mother Mary</u> gracefully moving to the front. The muted sound of soft music adds luster to her golden aura and the magic of her awesome presence.

"She hands me her rose, accompanied by a broad smile, that together represent everything she wants to share with me. No words are necessary. I pick up the thought vibrations and feelings flowing to me from the rose."

She tells me, "My child, we are all so very pleased with your progress. Many will depend on your sharing these messages. We also know that you are sharing them in your teaching, even though there are only a few.

"But this is all that is necessary, because you always share, and you never forget my message to heal the planet. You are keeping your promise as I asked you to, and for that we are all very grateful.

"But humanity shows no appreciation. They are not even aware that we want to help. Their level has sunken so low, it is beyond the density that we can reach,. Although we cannot reach them where they are, we have never stopped loving them. I know this because I lived a lifetime on your planet."

Christina asked, "You mean the soul."

And she said, "Yes. How can a mother not show love and understanding for her children? But they are all given free will. They can choose their own lifestyle, their own way of living."

Christina said, "But you still have this great love for all of them?"

And she tells me, "Yes. It is always great joy for me to see them coming home as free entities that are no longer inhibited by the physical body, or unwillingly bound to it.

"This is why we have love and understanding for all, but they must make an effort. They must want and need our love, and our help. Only when they ask, can we can help!

"Even though destruction will prevail one day. it is not looked upon here as it is seen by those on your planet. We see only a final freedom for souls of our children to return back home. The physical body without the soul is lifeless. It can then only serve as building material for the planet again."

Christina said, "I see the analogy you are giving me. Our physical body, without the soul, returns to the earth to fertilize the soil. Its only value, the chemical ingredients it will release into earth's soil."

She tells me, "When perceived in that manner, many think there is nothing greater than their physical body, and pamper and enjoy it as much as possible. With no thought of ill consequence, they stuff it with all manner of harmful edibles and other untested materials. Then they have to pay the price with ill health and an early demise."

She tells me, "In order to sustain your lifestyle on your planet, you must have the physical body. It is like a flower that cannot grow without being planted in the earth. It has to have good earth around it in order to grow. A seed alone cannot grow, a root alone cannot put forth additional root without the good earth to nurture it.

"Only then can it become wholesome and grow. This is how it is with your body. Yet you are the earth surrounding your soul. You are well aware how your earth has been polluted and poisoned, and many parts of the planet can no longer produce wholesome food.

"This is how it is with your physical body. It has been poisoned and polluted to the point that your soul no longer has a chance to grow and develop while housed in that body. And this is a very sad problem for us.

"It troubles us that this soul that was so much looking forward to learning many lessons about life on earth, has no chance at all for it is in a polluted environment. It feels the pain of the body. It is very much aware of all its illness. It cannot reach out and help because the physical body is not asking it for help.

"It is asking for help but on the wrong level! It is asking for help with the wrong kind of foods and lifestyle when it desperately needs the spiritual food first.

"This is why the cells in your body, the entire cellular structure of your body has been poisoned for eons of time. and has comparatively fewer healthy cells left. And even those few are slowly being destroyed by each generation."

Christina asked, "So, in other words, you are calling this self-destruction?

And she said, "Yes!"

"Oh, Mother, if only more people could hear what you just told me. I think many of them would pause for a while and think about it. No one wants to voluntarily create a sickly body. No one wants to be sick."

She tells me "They all have the same choice little one. It is never too late to change. We are always here to help, and to forgive. We hold no grudge, but they must want to change. They must want our help. It is only then that they can become strong.

"It is the only way they can become our help, our support, our soldiers like the few of you are. You have become very strong. and for that we are well pleased. This is what you promised when you came into this life."

Christina said, "I only wish I knew what all I had promised,"

And she smiles, "Oh, you impatient little girl. As you go

along on your path, you will become very much aware of what you have promised. For it is best that you learn one thing at a time. Then you do it in a very calm and loving way.

"If we give you the knowledge too much and too fast, you will become discouraged. We are all very much aware of this. You <u>are</u> in the human body in order to help us. Someone from earth must ask before we can help. You have asked, and we are helping your planet because of you.

"You are not just working with your spiritual body, you still have your physical body to work with as well. We are very much aware of everything, of all you are doing, your thinking, your dealings, and we have great understanding."

"So what is there to fear Mother?"

And she said, "Only the word itself, Everything is so easy and simple. You are the ones who find it difficult."

She tells me, "Most of this deals with the pollution of the cells, of the genetics and of course that involves your brain."

"And she tells me the brain that we are using is but a fraction of what we should have. The rest is all but dead and non-functional! So if we would use only half of our brain, we would still be on a much higher evolved level. That shows us how little we are using."

Christina continued, "And she is telling me that it has to be the right side of the brain. Do you mean a right and a left or just a right side of a brain?"

And she tells me, "Whatever you want to think of, whatever feels right. There are two sides of the brain, but they must function together with harmony, balance, and purity. The more we are living and thinking and working with the purity and the harmony of our brain, the more we can raise our own levels into a higher, spiritual one.

"She tells me, "The brain is highly evolved, but because of poison, wrong thinking, and wrong lifestyle, our brains are nowhere near what they should be. But there are brain cells that are still functioning.

"Your body is a perfect vehicle, as a means of transportation, to take you through this entire life cycle. This was the purpose for which it was created in the beginning. But you have created this brain and other damage to yourselves because you didn't want to listen to the right part of the brain. The right brain is your connection to the spiritual part that is your soul and its connection to creation.

"Your body should never get ill, should never become weak or out of balance for this is how it was created, perfect, like your souls! It is like children that are not being raised properly. They are becoming the product of what they have been taught.

"It can be likened to fertilizing the fields to yield a larger crop at harvest time. You will harvest the product you deserve, depending upon the degree of care and nourishment you gave it.

"If not cared for properly, it will grow as an abnormal crop, its form disfigured and unhealthy. In other words, as in this case your brain, the fertilizer we would use would be its spiritual contacts with the higher levels."

She tells me, "I can see in your mind that you are so right in your understanding. You understand me very well. I have to explain very little to you.

"You see, my child, when you are on this level with us, you open up to the level where you should be, where you can understand more through our vibrations and our thought forms than through our words."

Christina says, "Ah, Mother we are so unbelievably

dense.

She tells me, "I have such great love for everyone. Without this love, we could not be on the realm where we are. Without this forgiveness, without this kindness, no one would benefit."

She tells me, "I am so happy that you have chosen this right path. Stay on this path. Become as strong as you can, become as pure as you can, become as balanced as you can, then you can soar to heights you never dreamed of.

"Then you can make a great difference on both levels and I know you are able to be whatever you want to be. You are a very strong soul. You are also a very strong physical body.

"And you see, it does not matter how old you are, or how young you are. What matters is what you are within, in both the physical and spiritual bodies. Remember that, little one, remember!"

Christina said, "Thank you Mother Mary. There I see her rose unfolding again. I pick up that I am unfolding more and more onto higher levels. I guess this is the symbol of the rose. I feel even more humble than ever before, because what I am learning lets me see how little and how insignificant we really are.

"How little or small of a human being we are on this planet, we are nothing compared to the spiritual body! I am not only humbled but also very grateful. Any thought of control or ego or power would never ever enter my mind. That is not only stupid, it is unproductive and destructive.

"I am picking up a fleeting thought, "You are learning very fast.""

Christina said, "I love you Mother!"

She tells me, "Same here. She is telling me to come back

whenever I can."

She is leaving us again, slowly moving off to the right side of the stage. The intensity of the meditation that holds us in its arms reaches its highest level when in the presence of the powerful angels.

We will linger long and happily in our easy chairs, filled with the radiance of their presence and the magic of their prophecies.

Much that we learned today acquaints us with the present deterioration of earth's life-sustaining capabilities. and frailties of the human body that render it an easy target.

They are preparing us for the final message from Mother Mary and the Angels.. But they are also promising us a way to survival. Both possibilities have been or will be fully explained. The path we take is ultimately up to each of us. We still have the free will to choose.

Chapter XIX

What Might Have been

Christina said, "As I am floating through the door into the temple, I see many different beings, that are floating individually in the open area above the auditorium seats. Each of them is humming a soft, melodious tune that surrounds me.

"Such happiness is here, joy, and a wonderful feeling of belonging, of being included in their love, care, thoughts. and melodies. How lovely! It is an everlasting, flowing, weaving, surrounding of whatever feelings you can imagine!

"I am sitting down and taking a rose from the back of my chair. This fragrance always leaves me breathless, speechless.

"Now I see the <u>Master Healer</u> coming. He is putting his hand on top of my head."

He tells me, "My child, we are all pleased with your commitment, and that you are keeping the promise you made while still on the physical side. We see you giving everything you are able to give, do, say, or stand for.

"That is totality, and unless you make a total commitment it cannot be effective. It cannot be just a part of it, for it has to be all. It must be all or it cannot have an effect at this level. The effectiveness from our side can only come from enough help from all of you from your side. It must be everything or it will not be effective.

"Yet it must be a sincere effort from both sides. There can be no room for misunderstanding. We cannot have that and expect to succeed.

"Everyone must know there is a clear channel between you and us. As always, it must flow freely on the beams of the golden light of unconditional love between us. When your commitment flows under the bonds of that love, the bindings are unbreakable. You have made that commitment. Mother Mary and many angels have joined with you in that promise. to help you and those who work with you as long as there is hope.

"As long as you, and those that stand with you in this endeavor, work with us, we will stand with you from this side. Keeping your promise is all that is necessary. You, my child, have made a powerful beginning and we need many more like you to continue. And they will come because of you now, and other later.

"There are many others that also want to make a commitment, they want to help, and will once they find the way. You and others will be successful, for we will all be there and help until they are able to reach out to others, and others, and others. . .

"And I see it as a long chain that is just stretching everywhere and this chain will eventually stretch up to the Divine Plan and connect within the Divine Plan and, this is how many of you can make **the** difference for your planet. But we don't have years and years to do it. It must be now.

"You have the discipline, my little one. It will take all that you can muster to use it for yourself and pass it on to the others. They also must have discipline. This has to be a priority for nothing else matters!"

Christina said, "I hear Mataji coming. Thank you."

"There is no thank you necessary. There is only love and understanding necessary in keeping the promise. No words are necessary!"

Christina said, "I can see Mataji coming now. She has this brilliant light around her. She's just beaming at me."

Mataji said, "I was present last night, my little sister, and

I was very proud of your sharing your message, even though it has to become stronger. You must not waste time. The time is now more important than ever. You must keep the message only on what has to be done. You cannot waste time on anything else. For time flies, and it is so important that they understand everything that they should learn, to reach the level that you are on.

"They must learn in a short time to hear us, to feel us, to understand us. This can only be accomplished if they concentrate on this and nothing else. Discipline, my little one, is important, even as you have started to discipline yourself. Explain this to all others.

"Discipline is everything, and you must still become more disciplined. Without discipline we cannot achieve what we need in this short period of time."

Christina said, "I also feel the urgency, that we have such a short time frame. Unless we get this done in this time frame, I feel explosions happening all around me, and everything is disintegrating. Oh, my head hurts!"

And she tells me, "You are picking up my knowledge and my pain."

Christina said, "I really don't actually see anything, but I am picking it up through the vibrations."

And she says, "You are also picking up my thoughts. That is very good. That means that you have raised your vibrational levels even more."

Christina said, "She tells me how much she loves us, how proud she is of our effort, but we must make even more effort. She is reaching out her hands and touching mine and it feels like fire running up my arms, and running up and down my spine, and going up into my head. I don't know what this is for. It is like I can't even move."

She tells me, "This is part of your discipline. Now, with one thought you can activate the discipline within yourself, but you will have to learn how to use it. You have to discipline yourself with the discipline within yourself,"

Christina said, "Can I do all of that?"

Mataji said, "Yes, it can be accomplished now. You just have to practice, and than you will have maximum control of all disciplines.

Christina said, "Thank you. I will definitely work to improve it. She is just smiling."

Mataji said, "I know you will, for you like challenges, and you respond well to them. That is why you will accomplish much, and you are in the right place at the right time.

Christina said, "Thank you, Mataji. I know <u>Mother Mary</u> is coming for I can smell this sweet fragrance of roses.

"She is surrounded today by the Master Healer, Mataji, Michael, and Tschen Li. Even Joshua is there, with Mirva and Scarlet. It is like they are building a half moon around her and with radiant light that emanates from the group of angels that have come to be with her. Its like she is in the center of this half moon that is filled with a spectrum of all rays of sunshine."

Mother Mary said, "This is only a fraction of your spiritual family you see here, and many, many more are helping together to save your planet. We all are giving our energy, our love and understanding to your planet. These are only a few that are known to you, but there are many, many more! When you return home my child, you will remember them all, but for right now this is all you need to know.

"These are the ones that can help, and want to help.

They are the ones that can make the difference on your planet, and help humanity through what is to come.

"So you see, if we give our all we must have your all. Take note that there are only so very few from your side that are presently committed. This will have to do for the present, because more will come when they read my book and see how badly their help is needed.

"Because of our unconditional love, I and the angels you see standing behind me, will work untiringly with all of you, and do everything we can to save my children, even though there are those that cannot or will not hear and see. For they are all my children and I do love them, for some do not know. Some do not want to know!

"For most, their learning lessons will never take place on earth. When they return, they will take turns and learn these same lessons elsewhere, when they could have learned them during this lifetime. All they needed was the cooperation of the physical body to graduate from this life with all the necessary experiences.

"They could not graduate because the physical body was not willing to learn. The body was **not** willing to make the commitment or give up these lower vibrational pleasures. Yet, like many of them in their college lessons on earth, they waste their time on low level pleasures rather than study so that they could graduate and become a more intelligent being and go on to higher levels. They have done the same thing to the soul.

"So you see, my child, there is a simple explanation for everything. Simple enough for anyone to understand, but unless they have the discipline, unless they have the want, they cannot graduate."

Christina said, "I want to say they will always stay on

the lower levels, and eventually simply disintegrate at that level. In other words, that will be their reward."

She tells me, "Those that join all of you, that want to learn and raise their vibrational levels, their own souls will become overjoyed and happy. Once the soul is happy, that joy will filter down into the physical body and everything that is connected with the physical body will become this balanced oneness.

"The end result will be a one of happiness. There you will find peace and togetherness, with the soul functioning as it should be. When total balance is reached, harmony is achieved.

"When enough of you reach that level, our energy working with yours could produce the necessary correction to begin the healing of your own beautiful planet earth. Just imagine what powerful results that change could make. It is worth every bit of effort you put into it.

"This is why the soul level becomes our most important asset. It is the only way for you to know you have done the proper thing. You do not consult your physical level first. That is what is done by the majority of mankind, and is the reason earth is facing its present problem.

"I know that I have repeated this many times, but the reason is simple, you have to fully understand that this is the most important ingredient of your life. Soul level first, the rest will follow. In other words, if it does not resonate or jell within the soul level first, do not accept it.

"And discipline is very important. If it is a matter of feeding your soul level or feeding your physical level you will have to know which one to choose. And I believe you know this very well for someone else has shared this with you many times."

Christina said, "I don't know, I feel everything is so simple what you are saying. It's always simple when you are telling me. I don't feel that I have given all that I can, but I am willing to give more if it is needed. I don't feel that discipline is so hard to incorporate into our lifestyle."

And she tells me. "For you yes, for you have now committed yourself, my child, but it took you a long time."

Christina said, "Yes, I know. Because I now listen to my spiritual body more than my physical."

She tells me, "No matter how far you had fallen, there was always this little bit of spirituality there, always this certain something pulling you back up."

Christina said, "I felt it. It was always there. I don't know whether it was my spiritual body or not. I do know it was always in the back of my mind that there was something missing, that I was not doing what I should have done.

"And I used to get quite disgusted with myself. I don't know whether it was my upbringing during childhood, or whether it was my soul that was always trying to reach out to me. I guess I never shut the door all the way, it was always open so the soul could once in a while peek in and say, 'don't forget me.'" Ha, ha.

She tells me, "With the proper teacher, you were able to make the change with as many problems as you had. Anyone else can do the same, but they have to stop and listen within, and know that this is not just a body of flesh, it is a body that houses a spiritual body within.

"Without that spiritual body the flesh would be dead! Therefore, there are many like you in the times when you were down on lower levels, that need your help, and need you to open this little door inside of them so that the soul can start learning.

"So that the soul can start breathing out and ridding itself of all that darkness. Let that be your message, my little one, and you will know who that soul is. You will know who that person is. You must have enough discipline, and you must help them.

"You had Ralph to help you, and he promised Tschen Li and Mataji and worked with them. He kept his promise to them when he taught you. Now you have made a promise, and you will have to help them.

"Like Tschen Li and Mataji, they will help you now. Because of that, you have had their support. Now you have graduated, and now you must do that which you have promised, and do it on your own. All of us will be there to help you."

Christina said, "I am getting all this love from every one up here, it is like their approval, like they are very happy for me. It is like how could I ever go wrong with all of us standing here"

She is saying, "In other words don't ever, ever doubt yourself. We are here, and all will work with you. We know of your dreams, desires, love, and we know of your needs. We will be there to help in everything!"

Christina said, "So all I have to do is <u>do it</u>, and I will do it, that I promise. Thank you, every one of you! I get this feeling from Mataji, 'No thank you is necessary, only actions.'"

Christina said, "You don't fool around Mataji. do you?"

She said, "I never have."

Mother Mary continued, "But all of us work with such love that how can anyone ever take it in any other way. And love has to prevail in everything that you are doing. Love and understanding. Never be judgmental for you have no right to do that."

Christina said, "I understand."

She is saying, "This is the only reason I let you see how well-meaning souls, when on earth, can be deceived by the lower mind when controlled by the darkness. I see an important angel now entering the temple. Listen what he has to say when he tells you another part of the Divine Plan that is now happening. I will return a little later.

"Always be loving, and understanding in all you do from now on. We will never be far away. Use your vibrations and connect with us."

Christina said, "How simple it is just to connect with them and do what I can. Now I understand this part of the message you just gave me. I understood everything very clear.. and I will try to remember what this new angel has to say, and I will obey. And yes, I love all of you.

"The temple is now completely full. I had been standing. Tired but filled with energy, I resumed my seat. Mother Mary and the others had left. I waited for the angel who was to come. This promises to be an important message. I can feel the energy building all around me. I almost dare not to look ahead because of the strong vibrations I feel.

"I see this glowing master coming out, and I know that's the <u>Master of the Universe.</u> He has a brilliant corona and aura around him, as he is standing in front of me, I can now see him raising both of his arms. There is a wonderful glow coming out of every finger, and an aura around his hands that is almost blinding.

"As he is talking, he looks at us very sadly. I am picking up that the others in the universe can no longer help us. It has to stand by and let matters on earth take its course. In other words, the course of our planet. The universe cannot interfere,

"I feel that the help we could get from the universe would be great. But the universe can no longer help. According to the divine plan, it has to remain perfectly still and let the planet make its own adjustment and correction.

"I am being shown that the planet itself is slowly trying to crawl out of a thick level of darkness. The land area is totally smothered with it. And it represents everything bad and negative on our planet—the lust for power, greed, control, jealousy, the hopelessness, everything.

"It is being smothered so completely, you cannot see the surface of the continents. The land surface appears to be absolutely smothered with a darkness that moves slowly like a fog. And we are forced to exist under a thick blanket of suffocating air filled with something like thick soot.

"He is saying that it is so important to connect with the universe, with everything there is available. Only this spiritual connection can lift us above this level of darkness and enable us to breathe again and survive. Those that can make the connection with the universe will survive.

He tells me, "And the angels could stop this flowing mass with one thought, but they cannot interfere. They are sad it had to come this far. But they are also smiling, because they know the souls of those that perish will become free again.

"The souls are eager to return to our level.. They have been in a prison of earthly bodies for so long, they are no longer interested in anything earthly. It's no longer an issue. But with it decaying, the body will fall down to the bottom of the darkness and disintegrate."

Christina said, "That was quite an analogy, to really see that only the ones that want their help will receive it. That is awesome."

He said, 'No, this is the only way. This is the right way. Of course, it was only a vision that I gave you. But it is more than just a vision, it is also a promise. Just remember that and pass it on to others."

Christina said, "He represents all of the universe. He is the universe. He only appears to us to help us visualize his message better. But he's really a powerful glow of energy. All of this is so far over my head."

And he tells me, "Don't waste your time and energy trying to figure it out. Just try to understand."

"And now, I see him moving off to the rear. As he is moving away from us, the glow is becoming less and less until soon there is nothing left.

Now I see <u>Tschen Li</u> coming, he is wearing a white robe today. He says, "My children, you need the connection with the universe more than ever. You need help from all of us. It will be a difficult time. This time will continue into many years to come, just prepare."

Christina said, "And I feel that in the next few years, darkness will cover the land surface of the planet totally, and what I am being shown now is only the beginning. And once in a while, in this "Stuff." I can see a house, or an animal, or even a car or truck, in that stuff!

"It's almost like the flood they had way back when they built Noah's Ark. The way it comes to me is, it was not nearly as bad as this floating sea of darkness, making it difficult to even move. No matter how hard you try, you get stuck in one place or another. You are almost helpless.

"In other words, this time is going to be many times worse than it was with Noah. And when all of the cleansing has been completed, this darkness will almost disappear. I am being shown that this problem originated as the result of floods, volcanic eruptions, but most of all, through mankind's negative and evil thoughts.

Tschen Li tells me, "And it's going to happen so quickly no one will be prepared. No one will even be able to get help. It will come when it is least expected. So prepare, and be ready at any time.

"I will be there to help you with my energy. I will be there with many others, for you alone will not be able to accomplish everything."

"Now I can hear <u>Mother Mary</u> coming in. Ahhh, is she sad."

She tells me. "Nothing is worth doing without total spirituality—nothing. The rest is as worthless as the darkness covering the planet. Everything else is redundant.

"Mother is sitting in front of me, with such sad eyes, and tells me, 'You had to witness that. There is no other way of explaining it. This very same picture must be explained.'

Christina said, "Explained where, in the book?"

She tells me, "Yes, but also to all with whom you are in contact. They must be aware of the severity, for it has already begun.

"No matter how far away you look, it's there in all of its severity, extracting its mortal toll upon a materialistic humanity whose wrongful thoughts created its own exicutioner and brought it into existence, And in time it will slowly cover almost every part of your world."

"But, Mother, why this severity?"

She tells me, "There is no other way. Humanity had time but would not listen. Therefore, it has to be started anew. First, everything toxic, poisoned and negative has to be eliminated."

I am being shown, "As long as there is open water left, we will just swim or go by boat and rescue ourselves, which will teach us nothing. Only those that are on the spiritual path will be rescued."

Mother tells me, "Many of my children (souls) that are within every one of you have no chance to help in any way. for the average physical body does not want to help, know or learn.

"And now I see all of these red roses moving in mid air. Despite all of this disaster, her love is so overwhelming it disintegrates all that negativity. This is how powerful her unconditional love is. It is so awesome, I can't even express it.

"And she tells me, as long as you have high vibrations that is all you need. No need to express it, just feel it. Slowly she is moving back, off to the right. Oh, what a sad face.

"Oh, God, what have we done?"

In the somber silence that lingered long after her flowing blue cape faded into nothingness, the magnetic attraction of her spiritual presence held our minds as surely in her grasp as if she had remained in our presence.

Christina and I would remain seated in this Temple of Knowledge for a long time, as our minds reluctantly sorted through the startling revelations given us by these powerful angels.

When the time was right, while still in our altered state of consciousness, the angels that brought us here would slowly return us to the safety of our comfortable meditation room back on earth. Even then, we would remain in our present state of thoughtful reflection for a long time. Each of us would have scores of pictures of the day's revelations to paste into the album of our memory.

I remembered the promise Mother Mary made when we began this project more than a year ago. She promised that if we could interest enough people in the severity of earth's problem, and get them to work with us, we had a chance to prevent the inevitable correction earth itself would make in order to return to a healing balance.

From the nature of the human events that occurred during the past year, I have seen no improvement. In fact, the deterioration of human values continues to accelerate. In step with that decline, physical destruction of the objects of mankind's labor increases. All one has to do is listen to the weather reports. The sad facts speak for themselves.

In view of the above worsening conditions, if we are to succeed, we will have to get the angels' messages to those of us who are concerned as quickly as we can.

In his teaching, Jesus often used parables to help clarify the thoughts he wished to convey. The angels use the same pattern to help us visualize what they tell us. Only, they refer to their parables as analogies.

The parable they presented us today really brought their predictions to life. While their thoughts were not pleasant to hear, no one should doubt their sincerity.

Now it is up to everyone of us to CHANGE, LISTEN, and take action. Go within and see, hear, feel, and try to understand and help correct this situation.

You have free will, choose any legitimate way you can find. But do something now, there is not much time left. We will do all we can to help. Don't wait until it is too late. The angels' say, those who connect with them will be saved. As for me, I am taking their word for it.

We hope to see each of you in the temple of knowledge.

The New Beginning

Christina said, "I can already hear this wonderful choir. It is always such a sweet sound, such a joyful wave of melodies that penetrate my whole being. It is so angelic. That is the only way I can explain it.

"It comes enveloped in overwhelming love, a sensitive emotion of floating nowhere and everywhere. It is a feeling of weightlessness that dissolves into nothingness, yet you are everything. It is so hard to explain. But they are always so happy to see me and it seems as if they are always expecting more of us to come. This time it's only me.

"Perhaps others come occasionally, but for now they are very sad. This location is here for everyone. They are telling me that our souls could learn much more and evolve much higher while we are still on our side in the physical body. This could only be to our advantage, for then when we get back here, we can go to even higher levels. Everyone here is just anxious to grow and expand.

"This is done with so much love. There is no greed or enviousness, just a constant flowing of understanding, love and acceptance. Oh, this feeling brings tears to my eyes. If only we could have a fraction of this feeling on our planet.

"I think of yesterday. We sadly received the final message for this book. Of course it is not final to us who have learned to come to this level. We will continue to come here often for a total immersion in love and healing.

"It will not necessarily be final to those who read this book, for there will be several more to come. If enough concerned people join us, together we can make a great difference and alter the pattern of self-destruction that has brought us to the point of crisis.

"But how many will be enough? Each of you in your own heart will have to determine that for yourself. Mother Mary has said that we can still make that difference. They, of course, will always be ready to help.

"Well, I am floating on down to the front again. As usual, there is a red rose on my chair, how lovely. It never has any thorns. It is perfect! I am hearing the harp, jubilant and joyous, full of love and happiness.

"I see Master <u>Tschen Li</u> coming towards me. He is wearing a suit, not a robe. He says he is joining Joshua to help fight the battle on our planet. He has been chosen for that position and he is also telling me that he needs our help. I feel that he will support Joshua in doing back-up work.

"I am getting there will be some kind of diplomatic involvement, and I feel that he is going to be walking the face of the earth in an ordinary suit of clothes. He will be in his human body, and I am so grateful."

He said, "We will connect on many levels, many times in the future. I will need all of your help."

Christina said, "There is <u>Joshua</u> with his cape again."

He tells me, "Both of us have been chosen for this task and, as you know, we will walk right through everything! We will have no pity on the negative forces!

Christina said, "I have this feeling like it is either that way or no way. They seem to be very stern!"

He tells me, "Those that need to be dealt with will be taken care of, and those that are worth saving will be saved. But we do need your human energy. We also need your vibrations. Only then can we be effective for our vibrations can only reach so far. If you come up from your level to our level, to where we can meet, only then can we be effective on both levels.

"Since many of you have promised, and with more to come, it will work on both levels. And when we meet on this level and lock in, it will be like a magnet that nothing can penetrate! Nothing!"

Christina said, "I always get this feeling like when he pulls out this sword, he is just going to slice right in there! Oh my God! He doesn't even have a smile on his face, he is so serious, he is almost, I don't want to say angry, he just knows what he is going to do and he is going to do it! But he is going to do it with love and understanding."

"Well, of course," he tells me, "that is the only way. You forget what level you are on! 'I guess I have been told.' It can only be done with fairness, with love, with understanding, with purity, and balance. Also remember this sword is only a symbol of light on our level, nothing more."

Christina said, "He is finally smiling at me."

And he tells me, "I do have such faith in you, and Ralph, Sharon, Gregorio and George. There are many others that you are not aware of, but that is not important. Remain strong on your level, so we can always count on you. Of course, you always have free choice.

"Do not forget, little one, you always have free choice. It has to come from all of you with totally free will, and unconditional love! We are not asking for anything unless you want to give freely. Only then can we conquer all that we need to conquer."

Christina said, "Can I ask a question?"

Tschen Li looks at me and said, "I already know."

"Well, I want to ask it anyway. Does this mean that maybe we can . . .?"

He tells me, "This is not important now, whether we can

meet or not. But you will know when this will happen. You will know who I am, for you will pick up me vibrations!"

Christina said, "He is beginning to move to the back and is disappearing. I can see why. <u>Mother Mary</u> is coming in now! She has this blue veil just floating around her body. She also has a red rose in her hand. How lovely."

She tells me, "I am happy that you continue to come. Now you have heard from other angels. It is time to walk this path. It has begun! There is no other way, and time has gone by and there is little time left! And you will be my very close link that I will need for My Book to get out to humanity. You, and those working with you, are my hope, and I know all of you will do what you promised.

"This book will be the last hope for your planet. You have to believe in it! There is nothing else as strong as this book. Many will feel my vibrations with this message. And many are waiting."

Christina said. "I am picking up from her thoughts that if it were not for the unconditional love she has for mankind, disaster could have happened long ago. Her love is keeping the dark energy at arms length, or away from a very danger-us level that could destroy much! It is her love that is keeping this level of darkness away from all of us, as if she knows we all will take heed of things once we understand.

She says, "Why can't more pick up our vibrations and messages that we send to your planet daily? Why do they only pick up the low vibrational level? Why have so many fallen so low? It hurts me to see all this darkness that is just inundating your planet to the core, when there is no need."

She tells me. "You see, my little one, what you are being trained to tell them is the only way humanity can either grow to the level they should be, or they will have to take their consequences. There is no in between. It is either this way, or no way.

"The sad fact is that nobody wants to accept this warning. They have been bombarded with so much false doctrine, no one knows what to believe anymore. With all of that, they have thousands of reasons for not believing what I tell them."

And she tells me, "All of you have to be devoted. You have commit yourself. Only then can your soul gain the strength to soar to these higher levels amd work with us, then we can make a difference.

"It is so important to raise your vibrational levels for only then can we reach you and help. You will need this help, but you have to come to this level first! If enough of you do not reach this level, there can be only little hope!"

She tells me, "Your heavenly Father is in great pain. He wanted your world to become this paradise for all humanity, like the others that have succeeded. But your people have abused it so badly. If we do not succeed in reaching the people with My Book, there is little hope. He will not tolerate anything but a paradise, and he has been patient. He has been waiting, there are limits within the divine plan.

"There must be divine order. We are thankful that you have come back. I know you will follow through, for you have great strength within you. You know I have great love for all of you! Humanity must change to become this strong, unselfish and kinder planet again."

She tells me," This love has prevailed even in your darkest hour. You always knew to make the right decision at the last minute. Now you know why. I have been waiting for you to reach this level so that I can once again share this love with you. Soon we can be at this level forever!

"Remember, you will never have to face this alone. You will have me and many other angels to help you. The more you can tune in to us, the more you will know how strong you once were, the more your confidance will grow. After you reach this level again, everything will be very clear. The more you open up, the more you will remember. After that, nothing can stand in your way! Nothing!

"There will be this other strength beside you, that is so very important! This is why this book has already been approved by everyone here. We are only waiting for you to finish! Just do it! Everything is working according to the Divine Plan, and the Divine Plan is working in full force and nothing can change that.

"You are in perfect balance and harmony now. However, there is one level that you have not attained balance yet, so keep on reaching for even higher level, only than can you understand without a doubt."

Christina said, "Now, she is showing me this red rose."

And tells me, "This rose will always be my symbol of love. Do not forget. Visualize this red rose, and I **am** this rose. I will be in every rose even though you cannot see me, just feel me. This rose can be the symbol on all levels of love, You can become this rose with these perfect petals, by just visualizing."

Christina said. "I will share this powerful symbol of love with all that want to hear, know, and use it. For I know it will have a peaceful and loving effect on many. That will be my promise to you, Mother.

"This will be our protection and our strength, for many will try to penetrate, and harm us. It is also a protection, amd therefore fear should have no meaning. There will be only love, balance, harmony, faith. I guess you kind of knew that."

Christina answers in her own version: "I have been using Mother's wonderful rose over two years. And can openly say, it has become my symbol of spiritual love and protection. I use it within myself when I need healing, as well without for balance. <u>And it works. and is powerful.</u>

"Therefore, one cannot allow anything to penetrate that is even remotely connected with negativity! For that will take away the energy of life, love, harmony, and balance.

"Nothing is every worth it. For all is connected with the Divine Plan! It cannot be interrupted. If it is, it could mean major problems everywhere."

"Mother is telling me to always be mindful of the whole circle. This could be the difference between being saved or being destroyed! In other words I get this feeling, Mother, that when we share this message with all our friends, we have to be very clear and unequivocal. Either it is done the Divine Plan way, or no way!

"She just nods her head. In other words, the time to play around with and explain has elapsed. We did not adhere to it when we first got the warning signs, many years ago.

"All we needed to do was raise our vibrational levels and connect with spirituality, but greed, power, and everything else, has inundated our whole inner and outer being now there is no more room for that!"

She smiles and tells me, "You have not disappointed me. You could have started a little bit earlier with your promise. I also know you have learned your lessons well, and finally learned the right to be on this level.

Now she tells me, "It is time to reach the next level! You will know when this next level will be, only when you are in total harmony within and without. When the totality of all levels, of all feelings become a total oneness, then you have reached another higher level."

Christina   said, "In other words there is no end."

She tells me, "Precisely! This is spirituality, and when you are in spirituality there is no end. Everything is endless. You see my child this is why we live in this endless present."

Christina said, "I could not read this in any book."

She tells me, "Of course not, but everyone could have this same meeting and this pleasure. This book is to make the right ones aware of it. But if they still want to make the effort, or choose to make this commitment, I or the other angels would always be willing to come and help them. But most of all, to be again this Mother that I want to be for everyone. This is how much love I have! One day all of you will understand, when we are all united."

Christina said, "Oh, Mother, I do love you so much!"

She tells me, "I am happy with your progress on all levels. I approve of everything you are trying to do! You know that when it resonates within you, all will be well!"

Christina said, "She is leaving now with a red rose in her hand. My rose has again opened. It was closed at first, just a bud. What a little miracle. The meaning is clear, her love for mankind will open like her rose, for everyone who seeks and accepts her love."

THE END